get the most from your
COLES NOTES

Key Point

Basic concepts in point form.

Close Up

*Additional hints, notes, tips
or background information.*

Watch Out!

*Areas where problems
frequently occur.*

Quick Tip

*Concise ideas to help you
learn what you need to know.*

Remember This!

*Essential material for
mastery of the topic.*

Your Guide to ...

Bartending

How to mix over 100

drinks & cocktails

Setting up a bar

Party planning

ABOUT COLES NOTES

COLES NOTES have been an indispensable aid to students on five continents since 1948.

COLES NOTES now offer titles on a wide range of general interest topics as well as traditional academic subject areas and individual literary works. All COLES NOTES are written by experts in their fields and reviewed for accuracy by independent authorities and the Coles Editorial Board.

COLES NOTES provide clear, concise explanations of their subject areas. Proper use of COLES NOTES will result in a broader understanding of the topic being studied. For academic subjects, COLES NOTES are an invaluable aid for study, review and exam preparation. For literary works, COLES NOTES provide interesting interpretations and evaluations which supplement the text but are not intended as a substitute for reading the text itself. Use of the NOTES will serve not only to clarify the material being studied, but should enhance the reader's enjoyment of the topic.

© Copyright 1999 and Published by
COLES PUBLISHING. A division of Prospero Books
Toronto – Canada
Printed in Canada

Cataloguing in Publication Data
Abram, Stephanie Smith 1954–

Your guide to ... bartending

(Coles notes) ISBN 0-7740-0610-2

1. Bartending. 2. Cocktails. I. Title. II. Series

TX951.A27 1999   641.8'74   C99-930115-2

Publisher: Nigel Berrisford
Editing: Paul Kropp Communications
Book design: Karen Petherick, Markham, Ontario
Layout: Richard Hunt
Illustration: Jin X. Tang

Manufactured by Webcom Limited
Cover finish: Webcom's Exclusive DURACOAT

Contents

CHAPTER ONE

The basic bar

Setting up a home bar should not be a complex task. Stocking up on what you and your friends usually like to drink, plus a few "what ifs" for special occasions should be fun. Even planning a bar for a major celebration should not be a daunting task.

A somewhat more complex consideration is the ever-changing role of alcohol throughout history and, by extension, our relationship with alcohol today. As we move headlong into the twenty-first century we find social attitudes towards alcohol to be somewhat schizophrenic. Consider the following statements:

- Alcohol may improve cardiovascular health, yet …
- Alcohol is among the leading causes of preventable mortality, yet . . .
- Alcohol's history is as a popular drink, and a valuable source of fluid and calories, especially before the relatively recent availability of safe water, yet . . .
- It is estimated that 40 percent of the North American population is exposed to the effects of alcohol abuse through a family member, yet . . .
- Hundreds of millions of people drink responsibly at home and at social engagements.

As a responsible amateur bartender, you'll want to give some thought to the social and medical issues involved (see Chapter 11 for more on this), but you'll also want to have fun serving drinks and cocktails to your friends.

Water, water everywhere, but not a drop . . .

Until the nineteen century there was no way to provide a community with a limitless supply of clean drinking water as we have today. A community of any size very quickly polluted any drinkable water nearby, so drinking beer, wine or spirits was much healthier than sipping from the local well. A good indication of the importance of alcohol was the status it was granted in the Middle Ages as *aqua vitae* or *water of life*.

For most of us, to create a home bar and share alcoholic refreshments is to continue to take part in tradition: the tradition of being a good host, of creating comfortable and convivial surroundings, of celebrating social bonds. It is these traditions, probably more than the alcohol itself, that carry us through the gamut of alcohol-fueled celebrations, from backyard barbecues to marriage receptions.

The suggestions offered here should help you continue these social traditions and, perhaps, lead you towards starting some traditions of your own.

STOCKING YOUR BAR

Start with what you know you and your friends and family like, then work your way towards a larger collection. If you have a selection of liquors available to experiment with, who knows? You might even change your mind about what your favorite drinks are.

Initially, you might want to purchase moderate amounts in order to stretch your budget a bit further. Unless you run across one of those rare liquor-store sales or find yourself able to shop "duty free", 750 mL bottles are usually as cost-effective as larger bottles. Liqueurs are often cheaper than "hard" liquors and can be sampled in small bottles often stocked near the check out counter.

The starter bar

The stock suggested here should get you through a planned party or impromptu entertaining.

Liquor

brandy
gin
rum
scotch
tequila
vodka
whisky – Canadian, Irish,
   American or rye (choose 1)

Liqueurs*

Amaretto
Cointreau
Crème de Cacao
Crème de Menthe
Drambuie
Grand Marnier
Irish Cream
Kahlúa

* Choose three of four to start
  with, then add or replace with
  others as you see fit.

Wine and beer

apéritif wine (like Dubonnet
  or Campari)
beer (12 of your regular
  favorite, 6 lite)
champagne
  (or other sparkling wine)
red wine (2)
vermouth (1 or 2 small)
white wine (3)

Mixes

club soda
cola
cranberry juice
cream or milk
ginger ale
orange juice
pineapple juice
7-Up (or other lemon-lime
   soda)
tomato juice
tonic water

*Some items don't keep well. Vermouth, for example, needs to be refrigerated after opening, and even then doesn't taste the same after too long, so purchase smaller sizes and, hopefully, use it before it gets stale.

CONDIMENTS AND GARNISHES

If creating a really well-stocked bar is a priority for you, then there are some additional ingredients you'll want to have on hand: bitters (angostura is the most popular), coarse salt, lemons, limes, maraschino cherries, olives (small green, pitted), oranges, superfine sugar, Tabasco, Worcestershire sauce. Of course, plenty of ice is essential. Keep a good supply of cubes, then you can crack or crush as required.

GLASSWARE, GADGETS AND GIZMOS

Liquor alone does not a complete bar make. If you really want to do it up right, there is an array of bartending and serving equipment to choose from. Most general department or housewares stores will carry what you need. To check out what the pros use, try looking up **Bartending Supplies** in the **Yellow Pages** and arrange to visit a location. Here's where to begin:

Glassware You might be surprised to discover how many standard glasses there actually are. Don't worry about trying to stock them all – many bars don't either. Some experts suggest that all you really need are white-wine glasses and red-wine glasses. Other experts suggest that highball and old-fashioned (rocks) glasses are the minimum requirement.

Probably a compromise is best. Stemmed glassware is usually expected for wine and a longer stem is also useful for cocktails served without ice (the stem keeps warm hands away from the contents of the glass). Drinks that are served with ice, however, seem to require a more substantial base. Also, some of the most popular drinks are *tall* and really require the space of a good-sized highball, though it must be acknowledged that this space is deceptive since both a wine glass and a highball glass can hold about the same amount of liquid.

There is nothing wrong with multipurpose glassware. You can always collect more as you go along. Perhaps you should try to start with generous-sized wine glasses, highball glasses and something for beer (mugs or pilseners). Your house selections should, of course, be dictated by your tastes and habits.

Beer mug   Brandy   Champagne   Cocktail   Coffee

Collins   Cordial   Eggnog mug   Highball   Margarita   Martini

Parfait   Pilsner   Pousse-café   Punch cup   Red wine

Rocks   Sherry   Shot   Whisky sour   White wine

Hint Whatever style or size of glassware you decide to stock, the most important factor is that it be sparkling clean.

Beer mug A substantial glass, the handle of which should be big enough to accommodate your hand. The mug should hold about 12 oz. (375 mL). Both the thickness of the glass and the mass of the handle work to keep the beer cold.

Brandy or cognac These oversized, balloon-shaped glasses are meant to divert the aroma of a small amount of brandy or cognac towards the drinker's nose. The stems on these glasses are short since both the fragrance and the taste of the brandy or cognac are enhanced as the fluid warms in the drinker's hand. Size can run the gamut from 6 to 25 oz. (180+ mL).

Champagne flute The most popular style recommended for champagne, the flute is tapered towards the top to slow the bubbles. Other styles suggested for champagne include the saucer and the champagne tulip. Both have wider rims that allow the bubbles to escape more quickly. Flutes are usually available in the 6 to 11 oz. range (180 to 330 mL).

Cocktail The shape of this glass is so classic and familiar that it has passed out of the realm of mere glassware and into the land of universal symbol. It is meant for cocktails served without ice such as Manhattans, Stingers or Martinis. Generally, cocktail glasses are available in 4 to 6 oz. sizes (120 to 180 mL).

Coffee As its name implies, this type of glass is meant for those drinks that call for the addition of hot coffee: Irish Coffee, Spanish Coffee, Mexican Coffee. The handle protects the drinker's hands from the heat. Frequently exchanged as shower and housewarming gifts, they hold about 8 to 10 oz. (250 to 300 mL).

Collins This is a tall glass meant to accommodate a long, cool drink. In fact, sometimes this glass is called a *cooler glass* and is used for Long Island Ice Teas, Singapore Slings and Mai Tais, in addition to Tom Collins. Similar to a highball, it's taller, usually frosted and 10 to 14 oz. (300 to 425 mL).

Cordial (Pony) Meant for liqueurs, these small glasses can also be used for brandy and small pousse-cafés. Available in 1 to 2 oz. sizes (30 to 60 mL), they can also serve as shot glasses and jiggers.

Highball One of the most versatile glasses, the highball is meant for tall drinks on ice, such as gin and tonic, scotch and soda, and vodka and tonic. Sizes available range from 8 to 12 oz. (250 to 375 mL).

Martini In the cocktail glass family, the martini glass does not taper to a sharp V at the stem. It holds about 4 oz. (125 mL).

Parfait Though larger and flared at the rim, this glass is a type of pousse-café glass used for layered dessert drinks. Useful for layered desserts too – about 6 oz. (180 mL).

Pilsener Recommended as enhancing the taste of premium or light-bodied beers, the pilsener is an elegant glass, holding about 12 to 14 oz. (375 to 425 mL).

Pousse-Café A short-stemmed glass, typically with no flare to the bowl, this glass is recommended for layered dessert drinks. It holds usually 3 to 4 oz. (90 to 125 mL).

Punch cup A smallish glass with a handle. Probably the handle is favored as it slows the warming process of the glass and its contents. Possibly it is a throwback to some *help yourself* convention that we no longer follow. Generally, it is no larger than 4 to 6 oz. (120 to180 mL).

Red wine Although these glasses probably hold about the same amount of liquid as white-wine glasses, a red-wine glass generally has both a wider bowl and a wider rim. This is to allow the wine to **breathe**. Generally the bowl is a classic tulip shape and holds from 10 to 20 oz. (300 to 600 mL). It really shouldn't be poured more than half full.

One size does not fit all

There is a glassmaker in Austria, Georg Riedel, who insists that true enjoyment of wine demands a separate type of glass for each type of wine, i.e., individual glassware for Chardonnay, Bordeaux, Riesling, etc. He has created more than a dozen different designs so far. Riedel's theory has been born out by blind taste tests where experts have given one rating to a particular wine when served in the traditional tulip glass and then a different rating when served in one of Riedel's modified glasses. Food for thought, though perhaps not palatable to your pocketbook.

Rocks These versatile glasses are also called **old-fashioned** or **low-ball** glasses. They are meant for drinks served on ice, though they will also do for straight shots, brandy or liqueur, if you don't have a complete selection of barware. A single rocks glass holds about 6 to 10 oz. (180 to 300 mL); a double rocks glass holds about 14 to 16 oz. (400 to 475 mL).

Sherry A small wine glass, it could also be used for apéritifs, port, even liqueurs. It usually holds about 3 oz. (90 mL).

Shot An adaptable item, a shot glass can be used to serve liquor or to serve shots. Usually available in 1 to 2 oz. (30 to 60 mL) sizes. A shot glass used to measure liquor is often called a *jigger* and sometimes has measuring marks on the side. An actual jigger is 1½ oz. (45 mL).

Whisky sour Basically a cocktail glass, it is larger with a longer bowl designed to accommodate the foam of a sour drink. It generally holds about 5 oz. (150 mL).

White wine Similar to a red-wine glass, though often a bit smaller, the classic shape is like a tulip: a large bowl with a narrower opening to enhance both the taste and aroma. Usually about 10 oz. (300 mL).

It goes without saying that the range in quality of glassware is even greater than the range of sizes available. Full lead crystal, artisan blown, handcrafted, hand painted, designer – these are only a very few of the options available. Will expensive glassware make your drinks taste better? Only you can decide.

Gadgets and gizmos Likely you'll have some of these items in your household supplies. If you don't have a built-in bar (and most people don't), you might want to set aside a designated spot in a drawer or cupboard to house bar supplies so they are readily accessible. Most of the items suggested here are available in a wide variety of places, from discount department stores to specialty stores. Bartending supply places are always fun to visit, as are party supply depots. Also, don't forget the appropriate specialty magazines that are full of telephone or e-mail order possibilities.

Boston shaker Standard shaker Jigger Measuring spoons Bottle opener

Measuring cup Corkscrew Strainer Champagne stopper A waiter's wine opener

Mixing glass Citrus reamer Ice bucket and tongs Paring knife

Barspoon

Churchkey or can opener Muddler Glass pitcher Cutting board Blender

A few words about what's out there . . .

Barspoon A long, usually twisted handle, 10–14 in. (25–35 cm), with a flat bowl end. It can be used either for stirring or crushing ingredients.

Blender Nothing beats an electric blender's power for whipping up a frothy cocktail, alcoholic or otherwise. Try to get one powerful enough to crush ice.

Can opener A hand-held combination can-and-bottleopener is essential for your home bar and, unlike the blender, electric is not the better choice.

Cocktail shaker Essential equipment for cocktails "shaken not stirred." Of course, any savvy 12-year-old could tell us that this is how James Bond prefers his martinis, though there are several other drinks made in this style: sours, flips, gimlets and slings to name a few.

A professional bartender's shaker, also known as a *Boston shaker*, has two parts, a glass mixing portion and a metal portion. Both parts are flat-bottomed and the rim of the glass part fits inside the rim of the metal part so that a number of ingredients can be combined over ice. A word of warning: wet things get slippery, and a common bartending mishap is to lose control of the glass portion of the shaker.

Another type of shaker is the *Standard shaker*. This type consists of a large flat-bottomed container with a lid and strainer that attach. Some care is needed here to make sure that the parts don't fly apart while shaking. (*Handy hint*: Carbonated ingredients should never be included in a shaker. The results can be explosive.)

Corkscrews The type most recommended by professionals is the waiter's wine opener, a combination blade, corkscrew and bottle opener. Many people find they fumble with this, and prefer a wing-type corkscrew for home use, as it is more consistently reliable for the non-professional. There are other innovations available – pneumatic, electric and lever powered – so feel free to choose the tool that will make your life easier.

Cutting board and knife A small board and sharp knife will be useful for making fresh garnishes of fruit and vegetables.

Ice bucket and tongs Especially for a party, an ice bucket looks nice, it contains the mess to a designated area, and tongs are more sanitary than allowing everyone to touch the ice.

Jigger Though there are other ways of measuring liquor, this is by far the most reliable. Often double-headed, the larger side should measure 1½ oz. (45 mL), and the smaller side should measure 1 oz. (30 mL). This type is known as a jigger-pony combination, as a jigger is 1½ oz. and a pony is 1 oz.

Another useful type of measuring device is a small glass, metal or plastic container with marks indicating several points from 1/4 oz. (8 mL) up to 3 oz. (90 mL).

Measuring spoons Many drink recipes include the measurement of ingredients by teaspoon or tablespoon. It is handy to have two sets available, one for wet ingredients, one for dry.

Muddler A small pestle-like tool, preferably made of a hard wood, used to crush fruit or herbs and sugar.

Pitcher A nice touch for serving water or any other liquid that might be needed in quantity.

Strainer The most popular type is a Hawthorne strainer. This tool has a large spring coiled around its head and should fit snugly inside a Boston shaker's glass. Holding the strainer firmly inside the glass allows you to strain a chilled drink – without the ice – *straight up* into a glass.

Add-ons Your drinking habits, and those of your friends, will dictate which tools are must-haves and which are optional. Other items you might want to consider, especially for a social gathering, include:

*   an electric ice crusher to save wear and tear on your blender
*   a juice squeezer – essential for the purists
*   a set of matched bowls to hold garnishes such as cherries, olives, fruit wedges
*   a speed pourer (This replacement for a bottle top lends a professional touch to tending bar at home. If used correctly, it permits shots to be poured without a jigger, as each count of "one thousand and one" should equal 1/2 oz. (15 mL). The technique requires practice, though, before you try it in prime time.)
*   stirrers and straws (These more-professional items are available in a variety of styles, from disposable to designer.)
*   stoppers – useful for saving partially used items; there are special stoppers for wine and champagne
*   a wine cooler – both practical and elegant

Shake, rattle and roll

The concept of shaking liquids together in a specialized container can be traced at least as far back as 7000 BC to South America, where jars made of gourds were valued for mixing. Shakers as we know them today weren't really popularized until the nine-teen century, yet by the turn of the century, they became a standard tool of the trade. The twenty century saw cocktail shakers in a dazzling array of decorative, yet practical, designs. Stephen Visakey, of New York, has amassed a collection of almost 2,000 shakers and has also written a book, *Bar Ware, Identification and Value Guide*.

A museum exhibition of his collection includes shakers shaped like penguins, legs, bullets, bells, a golf bag and a fire extinguisher.

CHAPTER TWO

Beyond the basic bar

There is an art involved in mixing drinks. A large part of the art depends on the liquid assets, the glassware and the tools, of course, but there also seems to be a certain degree of magic.

In much the same way that some people always cook a perfect roast, or others pick the best mutual fund, some bartenders seem to produce the perfect drink. Of course, even professional bartenders often have quite specific specialties. This is why certain drink and mixology debates rage on. What exactly is the perfect martini? Should it be shaken or stirred?

Luckily for us, drink mixology is a topic people enjoy talking about. It is a field of endeavor that encourages sharing knowledge, not hoarding it. Indeed, this is so much the case that it is not hard to locate professional bartending tips in many formats. There are magazines, books, Web sites, even TV shows, all dedicated to demystifying the methods (see Chapter 12 for more on this).

Here are some of those little details that should help make the most of your efforts.

GARNISHES

Most garnishes serve two equally demanding masters – palate and presentation – so attention must be paid to both. Some professional bartenders call the purely decorative items garbage. This may be literally true, but it doesn't seem to capture the spirit of the total drinking experience.

Fruit garnishes Certain items should just always be on hand. Cherries, olives, lemons and limes are not hard to keep in stock. Parties or other social occasions might require additional garnish supplies, sometimes for flavor, sometimes for form, sometimes just for fun.

Cherries Maraschino cherries are the all-time favorite. Sold in bottles, they are generally found in the relish section of your grocery store. Most people prefer red cherries, although they are available in green for an unusual touch. Likely the cherry will be eaten and the ones with the stems make for civilized munching. Cherries are expected to be found in a wide variety of drinks from **Shirley Temples** to **Manhattans** to **Prados**.

Lemons An extremely versatile, must-have ingredient, lemons can be cut into wedges, slices or round wheels. The peel can be cut into twists or spirals. Conventional bartending wisdom dictates that any drink with club soda calls out for lemon. A **gin and soda** should be served with lemon.

Limes As versatile as lemons, limes are also popular additions to Corona, a Mexican beer. Conventional bartending wisdom dictates that limes go well with drinks with tonic water in them. **Gin and tonic** should *always* be served with lime.

Melons Cantaloupe, honeydew or watermelon make innovative and aesthetically pleasing additions to summer drinks. Indeed there are drinks called **Melon Ball**, **Melon Ball Sunrise** and **Melon Colada**.

Oranges Useful for their flavor additions to some tropical and sour drinks, oranges can be prepared in the same ways as lemons.

Pineapple Many tropical drinks conjure up the image of pineapple speared, sliced, or chunked. Think **Colada**.

Strawberries Found in punches and specialty drinks, perfect strawberries also look nice perched on the rim of a glass, or sliced in a drink. Some **Daiquiris** are made more appealing this way.

Preparation tips: Dried, shriveled or "off" fruit garnishes aren't worth using, so only prepare in advance small portions of what you will need to get started. Always wash fruit before preparing it.

Twists This technique will work for lemons, limes and oranges:

- Take a slice off both top and bottom of the fruit so that you can see the inside.
- Cut through the fruit peel from top to bottom.
- Slide a barspoon or sharp knife between the peel and the fruit to separate the two.
- Carefully pry the entire peel from the fruit.
- Cut the peel into thin strips from top to bottom.
- For a drink *with a twist*, rub the outside of the peel around the rim of the glass, twist the strip over the drink and drop it in.
- This process ensures that the essential oils are evident in the drink.

Slice Again, the same technique works for all:

- Cut thin slices off the ends of the fruit, then cut the entire fruit in half, top to bottom.
- Lay each half flat side down and cut half-circle-shaped slices.
- Some prefer to cut these slices in half again. In order to balance the fruit on the rim of a glass, cut just through the fruit slice, but not through the peel.

Wedges Some drinks call for wedges of fruit:

- For lemons or limes, cut the fruit in half, top to bottom.
- Lay the cut side down and slice in half again, top to bottom, then cut wedges from the quarters.
- For pineapple, slice off the top and bottom, then cut the fruit in half, from top to bottom. Slice each half in half again and carve away the core section. Now cut wedges.

Other Garnishes

Celery Synonymous with **Bloody Marys** and **Caesars**, a stick of celery, usually with the leaves still attached, is *de rigueur* for drinks with a strong vegetable-juice mix.

Cucumber A curl of the peel or a thinly sliced wheel of cucumber is often suggested for drinks with **Pimm's** in them.

Mint Leaves One of the key ingredients of a **Mint Julep**, sprigs of mint are also fragrant additions to some punches and summer drinks.

Olives These are part of the **Martini** mystique. No bar, no matter how small, would be complete without them. Keep small-to-medium *green* pitted olives on hand (black olives are too strong). It's best if they are kept in your fridge as they'll last forever and taste better.

Onions Pearl onions are another popular garnish for **Martinis** (though garnished with an onion, it is called a **Gibson**). These tiny onions are available in jars and will last as long as olives if refrigerated.

Condiments

There are a few additional mixed-drink ingredients that most people stock in their cupboards anyway. These are items to set out or have at-the-ready for social occasions: bitters, black pepper, cinnamon sticks and ground cinnamon, grenadine, nutmeg, salt, sugar, Tabasco sauce and Worcestershire sauce. Superfine sugar, also known as fruit sugar, dissolves most easily.

Bitters is an interesting ingredient frequently called for in a vast array of food and drink recipes. The most popular type of bitters is

Angostura, apparently formulated as an appetite stimulant and tonic for soldiers in South America in the first quarter of the nineteenth century. The substance is itself alcoholic, so should probably not be served to any abstaining friends and relatives. Regardless of its medicinal roots, its unique combination of tropical herbs and spices is valued now for its flavor, best appreciated by the drop or dash. **Pink Gin**, for example, is just gin with a dash of bitters.

There are other types of bitters. Orange bitters is a frequently listed ingredient. Also, for spicy Cajun-style drinks there is Peychaud's Bitters, from New Orleans.

SECRETS FOR SUCCESS

Actually, there are probably as many bartending secrets as there are bartenders, but when setting up a bar in preparation for an occasion, there are a few details to keep in mind to make your event run more smoothly.

- Bar **set-up** should be close to a sink and refrigerator, so likely it will be in the kitchen. Anticipate the supplies that will be used and have them out and ready. This is particularly true of garnishes, which are time-consuming to prepare on the spot.
- **Chilled** glassware is a really nice touch. You can accomplish this at home by putting the glasses in the refrigerator for about an hour before they need to be used. You can also accomplish the chilled effect by filling the glasses with cold water and ice for a short while before you serve drinks in them.
- To **frost** an entire glass, dip it in water and put it in the freezer for at least half an hour. To **frost the rim**, run a wedge of lime or lemon around the edge of the glass and dip it in either sugar or salt.
- **Refrigeration** is also a recommendation for liquors and liqueurs that will be used in cold mixed drinks. Vodka, for example, is even more delightful if stored in the freezer (its alcohol content prevents freezing, just like car antifreeze).
- **Ice** is a key feature of most mixed drinks. It needs to be fresh, perhaps even purchased in a bag so that you don't ruin a good drink with ice that is spoiled by that odd freezer odor that

sometimes occurs. If your ice is not fresh, or if you suspect somewhat smelly ice, try rinsing it under the tap to freshen it up. Make or buy more ice than you think you need. Use of ice always seems to exceed expectations, especially if you don't have room in your refrigerator to keep all of the other drink components chilled too.

 On the rocks means to serve a drink with ice. Many drinks are served **straight up** meaning without ice, yet they are frequently mixed with ice, then strained before serving.

- **Mixes** should, of course, be cold. Watch soda water, as it will explode if opened warm. Open it slowly over a sink. Most professionals will recommend using freshly squeezed juices. Try to at least buy them fresh and real, avoiding the artificial-flavor juices.
- **Bar mix**, also known as sour mix, is a component of several favorite drinks. This can be purchased in bottled or powdered form, or you can make it yourself with 12 oz. (375 mL) of lemon juice (the juice of about 6 lemons), 18 oz. (565 mL) distilled water, 1/4 cup (60 mL) sugar and one egg white. Simply blend all of the ingredients in a blender until frothy, or shake them in a large jar. Bar mix will keep in the refrigerator for about a week. In a pinch, you could combine the juice of half a lemon and 1 tsp. (5 mL) of sugar per drink, in a shaker, with all of the other ingredients. If shaken vigorously enough, the foam will appear.
- **Sugar syrup**, also referred to as simple syrup, is another frequently called-for ingredient. To make, dissolve 2 cups (500 mL) of sugar into 1 cup (250 mL) of water. Bring to a boil, reduce the heat and simmer, stirring until it has thickened. This whole process should take about 5 minutes.
- When should you **shake**, when should you **stir**? Generally, a

18

drink is stirred if there is no sour mix or cream involved, or if there are only a couple of ingredients. Do not stir soda or sparkling wines too much or they will go flat. A drink with one liquor and one soda, say **gin and tonic**, does not even need to be stirred if you pour the tonic on top of the gin – the bubbles will do the stirring for you.

Shaken drinks usually contain a number of ingredients or difficult-to-mix components, a **Gin Alexander**, for example. This is in contrast to a gin and tonic, which you could easily build with neither a stir or shake. Never shake a drink with any carbonated soda in it.

Most recipes will give instructions, or perhaps your guests will request one style over another. Although most martini recipes will suggest stirring, there are many people who prefer it shaken, like 007.

- **Measurements** shouldn't be a mystery. In fact, guesstimating amounts is probably least likely to produce the desired results. In addition to a standard jigger, pony and shot glass, you should also have on hand measuring spoons and a measuring cup. If a recipe calls for a **dash**, the required amount would be about 1/4 tsp. (1.25 mL). If 6 oz. of something is called for, this is measured as 3/4 of a cup (190 mL) and is also known as a **split.**

CHAPTER THREE

Planning for a party

Once you have decided to entertain, regardless of the occasion, there are a few practical details that you need to consider for setting up your bar.

SHOPPING LIST

Likely, the majority of your entertaining ventures are casual and revolve around wine, beer and a favorite liquor or two. The occasions considered in this chapter though, are those special enough to warrant a more prepared bar. This can involve a **full bar** with numerous liquors and mixes available or, perhaps, a **theme bar** with a few offerings specially thought out in advance.

A theme bar can work for both a large party and a smaller gathering. For a small gathering, you might want to create a bar according to the food that is being served or the time of the day. If you are serving nachos, tacos or fajitas, for example, you might want to limit your liquor offerings to tequila and Mexican beer. Sangria would be an appropriate offering with tapas and paella. Gin drinks would be a good choice for summer afternoon entertaining. Dessert parties are a good place to serve champagne, or liqueurs and specialty coffees.

A larger party can revolve around theme drinks too, especially if it's a theme party. One particularly popular theme is the tropical party. There are several delightful tropical drink concoctions you could explore (see Chapter 10 for several suggestions on this theme). For these occasions you will need to buy more than one liquor, but may not have to have as extensive a collection as a full bar set-up requires.

Next, let's consider the full bar. Hopefully, you are not starting from scratch. Your usual bar stock should provide you with a base (see Chapter 1). Stocking up for 10 guests is practically as costly as stocking up for 40. If you have leftover unopened liquor, it is more than likely that you can return it to the liquor store, as long as you have retained your receipt.

Liquor product	Small to medium Party	Medium to large party
750 mL bottles	10-40 guests	40-100 guests
brandy/cognac	1-2	2-3
gin	1-2	2-3
liqueurs	3 assorted	3-4 assorted
rum	1-2	2-3
scotch	1-2	2-3
vermouth	1 dry, 1 other	2 dry, 2 other
vodka	2-3	3-4
whisky	1-2 assorted	2-3 assorted
white wine	6	8-10
red wine	3	5
blush wine	1	2
sparkling wine/ champagne	4	6
beer	1 case for every 10 guests	same

This guide is general. Your shopping list will be affected by your knowledge of your guests and the occasion. Time of year is also a factor. Beer and the light-colored liquors are more popular in the summer. The dark liquors, brandy and liqueurs are more popular in the winter.

Of course, you'll need other supplies besides liquor. Mixes, garnishes and ice must be factored in also. Conventional wisdom dictates that you should have more of these items on hand than you think you need. Sodas and juices will be doing double duty, in alcohol and non-alcohol offerings alike. This is also true of ice. If you can double or triple the ice, based on what you think you'll need, that will probably be about right. No room in your freezer? Store bags of ice in your washing machine. They will stay frozen there for quite a while. Chest coolers work well too.

Product	Small to medium party	Medium to large party
	10-40 guests	40-100 guests
Sodas (2 litre bottles)*		
club soda	3	3-5
cola	6	6-10
ginger ale	2	2-4
lemon-lime	2-3	3-5
tonic	2	2-4
supply both diet and regular		
Juices		
cranberry	2	3
grapefruit*	2	3
orange	2	3
tomato	2	3
might substitute clamato, peach, pineapple		

The other miscellaneous supplies are consistent with basic bar set-up suggestions already given. Fresh fruit for garnishes, bitters, cherries, olives, cocktail onions, sugar, milk, cream, sugar syrup, bar mix (sour), Tabasco and Worcestershire sauces will all go a long way towards making your bar complete.

BAR SET-UP

Whether you set up a full bar or a more limited theme bar, basic questions need to be answered. Who will tend bar? Self service usually works for crowds of 20 or fewer. More than 20 guests and you might want to tend the bar yourself or enlist a friend to help. If your party is really large, you probably need a designated or professional bartender.

Where, and on what, will you place your bar supplies? There is no definitive answer here, but you do want an answer to this question. Some considerations will be traffic flow, proximity to water and, possibly, an electrical outlet for a blender or ice crusher.

What else should be on a bar? Cocktail napkins would be useful, as would a couple of towels and a cloth. Of course, your bar tools and glassware should be there. Do you have enough glasses? You could always borrow, rent or use plastic to round out your selection. There should be a garbage receptacle in close proximity to the bar.

Set up the bar in advance. Chill what should be chilled, and be prepared to continue chilling for the duration. Garnishes should be fresh, but they can be prepared and set out an hour or so ahead. If you are serving a punch, it can probably be at least partially prepared ahead. With enough planning and preparation, you might even enjoy your own party.

A self-serve bar

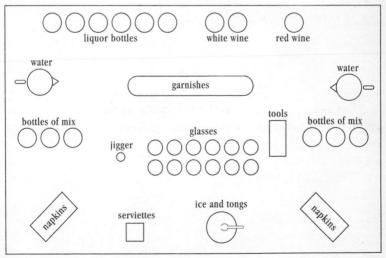

CELEBRATION SUGGESTIONS

While the full bar is one way to go, entertaining often revolves around specific celebrations and holidays. For these occasions it is perfectly acceptable to plan to serve your liquor somewhat like your food – that is, the selections are predetermined. Selecting your beverages can work for dinner parties as well as theme events.

You might, for example, be planning a dinner for eight, and the food will be Italian. Before dinner you could decide to serve Campari **apéritifs**. (Apéritif comes from the Latin word *aperire,* meaning *to open.* These are drinks taken before a meal. Classic apéritifs are Campari, Dubonnet, Jagermeister, Lillet and Pernod.) With dinner you could have both red and white wine available. After dinner you could serve Amaretto Café, or Amaretto, separately, with coffee.

This type of thoughtful planning cuts down considerably on what a host needs to have on hand, yet makes for an enjoyable event for your guests. Of course, it is usually a good idea to have alternatives for all kinds of reasons. Extra wine, beer and alcohol-free choices are important options to have on hand.

Apéritif appreciation

Any drink you serve before dinner qualifies as an apéritif. If you are looking for something classic, try these:

Americano: 1 oz. (30 mL) sweet vermouth, 1 oz. (30 mL) Campari, club soda, orange peel twist. Stir the vermouth with Campari and ice in an old-fashioned glass. Top up with soda and twist the orange peel in.

Duchess Cocktail: 1 oz. (30 mL) dry vermouth, 1 oz. (30 mL) sweet vermouth, 1 oz. (30 mL) Pernod, orange slice. Stir the liquids with ice and strain into a cocktail glass. Garnish with orange.

Planning your beverages and limiting your bar can work for other events, both large and small. Anniversary parties and showers are almost synonymous with punch. Brunches and dessert parties cry out for champagne concoctions, as do New Year's Eve parties. Après ski affairs call for warmed drinks, and Christmas means eggnog. There is likely a drink recipe suited to almost any occasion you might imagine.

THEME AND HOLIDAY DRINKS
Some suggestions to get you going:

Academy Awards Night Spend the night with two great ladies from the silver screen.

- **Mary Pickford:** Equal parts rum and pineapple juice with a splash of grenadine.
- **Shirley Temple:** See Chapter 11.

Brunch A good way to celebrate many festive occasions, from New Year's Day to Easter.

- **Bellini:** 1 very ripe peach, brut champagne. Purée peach in blender and pour into a champagne glass. Add ice-cold champagne. (This can be made for a crowd by puréeing several peaches at a time.)
- **Kir Royale:** 5 oz. (150 mL) brut champagne, ½ oz. (15 mL) crème de cassis. Gently mix cold champagne and cassis in a champagne glass.
- **Mimosa:** Orange juice, brut champagne. The proportions are up to you, but the ingredients must be cold.

Canada Day For a little patriotic fervor.

- **Bloody Caesar:** A made-in-Canada cocktail (see Chapter 7).
- **Canadian Cocktail:** 1½ oz. (45 mL) Canadian whisky, 1/2 oz. (15 mL) Cointreau, 1/2 tsp. (2.5 mL) superfine sugar, bitters. Combine all and shake well with ice. Strain into a cocktail glass.
- **Canadian Salad:** 1 oz. (30 mL) Canadian whisky, 1/2 oz. (15 mL) brandy, 1/2 oz. (15 mL) Irish mist, 1/2 oz. (15 mL) scotch,

1 oz. (30 mL) orange juice, 1/2 oz. (15 mL) lemon juice, 1/2 tsp. (2.5 mL) superfine sugar, orange slice, maraschino cherry. Reserve orange and cherry for garnish. Shake the rest with ice and strain into an old-fashioned glass filled with ice.

Christmas

- **Eggnog:** 12 eggs separated, 2 cups (500 mL) superfine sugar, 2 cups (500 mL) rum, 2 cups (500 mL) cognac, 6 cups (1.5 L) milk, 2 cups (500 mL) cream, nutmeg, cinnamon. Beat yolks and sugar until thick. Stir in rum, cognac, milk and cream, then chill. Just before serving, beat egg whites until stiff and fold into chilled liquid mix. Sprinkle with nutmeg and cinnamon, but do not add ice. This will serve about 10.
- **Poor Man's Eggnog:** Buy eggnog from store; add jigger of rum, garnish with nutmeg. Don't pretend it's the real thing – simply say you had to spend all your time trimming the tree.

Halloween

- **Black Magic:** 1½ oz. (45 mL) vodka, 3/4 oz. (22 mL) coffee liqueur, dash of lemon juice. Shake vodka with liqueur and cracked ice. Pour into an old-fashioned glass and add a dash of lemon juice.
- **White Ghost:** 1¼ oz. (38 mL) Frangelico, 3/4 oz. (22 mL) white crème de cacao, 1/4 oz. (8 mL) Chambord, 2 oz. (60 mL) heavy cream, fresh raspberry. Mix liquids in a blender with cracked ice until smooth. Serve in a chilled cocktail glass; garnish with raspberry.
- **Zombie:** See Chapter 5.

Leap Year You only need this one every four years!

- **Leap Year Cocktail:** 1½ oz. (45 mL) gin, 1/2 oz. (15 mL) Grand Marnier, 1/2 oz. (15 mL) sweet vermouth, 1 tsp. (5 mL) lemon juice. Stir all with ice and strain into a chilled glass.

Sports

- **Beer:** Enough said.
- **Golf Martini:** 2 oz. (60 mL) gin, 1 tsp. (5 mL) dry vermouth (to taste), a few dashes Angostura bitters, green olive. Stir gin, vermouth and bitters vigorously with ice. Strain into a chilled cocktail glass and garnish with olive.

St. Patrick's Day Everybody is Irish on St. Patrick's Day – or will think so after enough of the suggestions below.

- **Irish Coffee:** See Chapter 10.
- **Irish Magic:** 1 oz. (30 mL) Irish whiskey, 1/4 oz. (8 mL) white crème de cacao, 5-6 oz. (150-180 mL) orange juice. Stir all with ice in a highball glass.
- **Leprechaun's Libation:** 1½ oz. (45 mL) Irish whiskey, 1/2 oz. (15 mL) green crème de menthe, 1/2 cup (125 mL) cracked ice. Combine in a blender and serve in a stemmed glass.

Thanksgiving

- **Thanksgiving Cocktail:** 1 oz. (30 mL) gin, 1 oz. (30 mL) dry vermouth, 1 oz. (30 mL) apricot brandy, 1/2 tsp. (2.5 mL) lemon juice. Shake all with ice and strain into an old-fashioned glass filled with ice.

Wedding Drinks Also suitable for showers, anniversaries and receptions.

- **Champagne Cocktail:** 1 sugar cube, several dashes Angostura bitters, champagne to fill, lemon twist. Drop sugar cube into a champagne flute. Add bitters and then the champagne to fill. Stir gently until the sugar dissolves. Garnish with the twist.
- **Wedding Punch:** 1 L vodka, 3 cups (750 mL) orange juice, 1 cup (250 mL) lemon juice, 2 L ginger ale, cherries, lemon slices, orange slices. Combine vodka and juices and chill. At last moment, add ginger ale and a block of ice. Garnish with fruit. Serves about 10.

Kosher products, spirits, wines and beers are available, so ask at your local liquor store.

A WORD ON MAKING TOASTS

Social gatherings frequently require someone to say a few words. This is a practice as old as time, and these are thoroughly universal:

- Cheers
- Sköl
- A votre santé
- Prosit
- L'chaim
- Salud
- Kanpai
- Bottoms up

If you are required to say more than one of these basic selections, do not panic. An expression of your true feelings may be suitable, if your true feelings ought to come out given the company around you. If not, check out a dictionary of quotations. What others had to say about a particular subject might apply, or it might provide you with a launching pad. Check out your local library or bookseller too, as there are collections of toasts available. Don't forget the world at your fingertips via the Internet. A general search on the word "toast" will not be too fruitful, so limit your search accordingly. "**Wedding toasts**," for example, will be a much more successful search.

Here's a sampling of some of the gems you'll find:

If all be true that I do think,
There are five reasons you should drink;
Good wine – a friend – or being dry –
Or lest we should be by and by
Or any other reasons why.

– Henry Aldrich

Here's a health to all those that we love,
Here's a health to all those that love us,
Here's a health to all those that love them that love those
That love them that love those that love us.

> – *Anonymous*

Here's to your health,
and your family's good health,
and may you all live long and prosper.

> – *Joseph Jefferson*

May you live all the days of your life.

> – *Jonathan Swift*

Here's mud in your eye!

> – Casablanca *(1942)*

To love and laughter and happily ever after.

> – *Anonymous*

May you live as long as you want to, and want to as long as
you live.

> – *Anonymous*

CHAPTER FOUR

Gin

Since gin is possibly one of the most versatile of liquors, gin drink recipes are numerous and found in great profusion in most bartending guides. Interestingly, gin started life as a medicine.

GIN SAVVY: HISTORY, PRODUCTION AND STORAGE

Gin seems to be the only liquor than can be attributed to a single inventor. Franciscus de la Boe, also known as Dr. Sylvius, was a professor of medicine at the University of Leiden in Holland. Using what was known about the diuretic effects of juniper berry oil, the good doctor strove to create a medicine that could combat the kidney and bladder ailments afflicting sailors with the Dutch East India Company in the middle of the seventeenth century.

Although the combination of distilled alcohol and juniper berry didn't actually cure the sailor's ailments, the fragrant potion became immediately popular as a sort of general all-round tonic. If nothing else, patients quickly forgot their ailments, and the concoction was lauded for its properties as a sedative and appetite stimulant.

Logically, the Dutch christened this potion *jenever*, the Dutch word for juniper. As its use spread, the French called it *genièvre*, and the English shortened that to *gen*, then *gin*.

Apparently, English soldiers came across the drink when they were fighting in the Netherlands in the late seventeenth century. Discovering its many virtues, they nicknamed it *Dutch courage* and took mass quantities back home with them.

Almost simultaneously, William III, a Dutchman, married Mary II and became king of England in 1689. This king, also known as

William of Orange, drastically raised taxes and duties on all French wines and brandies. This act made Dutch gin much cheaper and more accessible. Then, in 1690, the English Parliament passed an act to encourage distillation of spirits from corn, so the English produced their own version of gin using corn-based spirits. English gin eventually evolved into the lighter, drier gin that is most popular today.

Unfortunately, gin was almost *too* popular in the eighteenth century, when it became practically the national drink of England. With more than 7,000 gin establishments in London alone, alcoholism reached near-epidemic proportions. It is estimated that in the mid-eighteenth century approximately 11,000,000 gallons (44,000,000 L) of gin were consumed annually just in London. Soon gin's soothing effects and emboldening properties became comingled with other less beneficial effects, and it earned the nickname *Mother's Ruin*. Living on *Gin Lane* was synonymous with an undesirable lifestyle.

Luckily, tea came to the rescue as a newly popular beverage, and gin consumption became more moderate. Gin was also saved from total banishment by the Gin Act of 1751, which regulated the sale of gin to only those establishments licensed to do so by the government. Nonetheless, a seedy bar is still called a *ginmill*.

Production Each type and brand of gin is slightly unique. All gins contain juniper and all "dry" gins also contain coriander seed. The combination of other particular ingredients can vary. Some of the botanicals that may be included are: angelica root, iris root, licorice, lemon peel, orange peel, almond, cassia bark, anise, caraway seeds, ginger, fennel, cinnamon bark and cocoa. The exact recipes are guarded secrets, so likely there are ingredients only a handful of people know of.

Gin is unaged, therefore, it was, and remains, a handy *bathtub recipe* liquor. Popular during Prohibition, bathtub gin recipes can be found today on the Internet.

Almost all gins are distilled twice. First a grain spirit is distilled, then that is re-distilled with juniper berries and other flavoring components. This process produces a **London dry gin**. There are also flavored gins and this will be noted on the label. A sweet gin does exist, known as **Old Tom**, though its lack of popularity these days makes it a rare find. It is thought that Old Tom was the type of gin used in creating the original Tom Collins. (This seems likely since a Collins recipe now requires the addition of sugar.) **Plymouth gin** is another type made in only one distiller and completely unsweetened. This has been the traditional gin of the British Navy and is thought to have been the gin used to create the original **Pink Gin**.

Storage An open bottle of gin should be fine for about two years, especially if stored in a cool, dry, dark space. In the summer you might want to keep gin in the fridge if gin drinks are a favorite in your home.

What about metric?

The astute reader will already have noticed that our drink instructions are given first in ounces and second in metric. Why? The simple answer is that the cocktail and the idea of measuring liquor are two very English concepts. A standard shot of liquor, as measured by a jigger, is 1½ ounces. This is roughly 45 mL in metric volume, an awkward measure to say the least.

The French are unaffected by this problem, however, since they rarely measure their liquor. Instead they pour *une dose* of however many millilitres of alcohol a drink might require. Of course, this requires a certain *savoir-faire*.

GIN CLASSICS

Now for the part you've been waiting for . . .

Unless otherwise stated, the following drinks should be made with a London dry gin. In drinks where the gin's presence will be prominent, it would be best to use a premium (expensive) brand.

Gibson

2 oz. (60 mL) gin
dash (or so) dry or extra dry vermouth
cocktail onion

Pour the gin and vermouth into a mixing glass filled with ice. Stir and strain into a martini glass or a rocks glass filled with ice. Garnish with the onion.

· ·

A **Gibson** is really a martini with an alternate garnish. The vermouth can be adjusted depending on how dry you want the drink to be. The drier the Gibson, the less vermouth is involved. Some go so far as to swirl a dash of vermouth and then dump it, before adding the gin; others spritz a fine mist of vermouth above the glass with an atomizer, if you can imagine!

· ·

Gimlet

1½ oz. (45 mL) gin
1/2 oz. (15 mL) fresh lime juice
pinch of powdered sugar
lime wedge

Combine and stir ingredients to dissolve sugar in a shaker glass filled with cracked ice. Shake and strain into a cocktail glass. May also be served with the ice. Garnish with lime wedge.

· ·

It is common to make a gin gimlet with 1/2 oz. (15 mL) **Rose's** lime juice. Since this mixture is concentrated and sweetened, the sugar above should be omitted. Invented in Scotland by Lauchlin Rose in 1867, Rose's lime juice was intended to stave off scurvy aboard ships. It quickly gained popularity and its acceptance by several shipping companies meant the product spread to wherever these ships travelled around the world. Rose's products are standard bar stock.

· ·

Gin and Tonic

1½ oz. (45 mL) gin
5-6 oz. (150-180 mL) tonic
lime wedge

Pour gin into a highball glass over ice. Pour in the tonic and garnish with a lime wedge.

Gin Cocktail

1 oz. (30 mL) gin
2 oz. (60 mL) dubonnet
dash of bitters
lemon twist

In a mixing glass, at least half full of ice, stir gin, Dubonnet and bitters. Strain into a cocktail glass and add the lemon twist.

Gin Fizz

2 oz. (60 mL) gin
1 tsp. (5 mL) superfine sugar
juice of I lemon
club soda

Combine first three ingredients in a shaker with ice. Shake well, then strain into a highball or Collins glass filled with ice cubes. Top it up with soda. You can also just add gin to a prepared sour mix.

••

The Gin Fizz is an old concoction dating back to the 1880s in New Orleans. The original is apparently attributed to Henry Ramos, owner and proprietary of the Imperial Cabinet Saloon. His creation also called for an egg white, cream, orange flower, lemon and lime juice, plus vanilla extract.

••

Gin Fizz (a variation)

  1½ oz. (45 mL) gin
  1 tbsp. (15 mL) powdered sugar
  3 oz. (90 mL) bar mix
  club soda
  maraschino cherry
  orange slice

In a shaker filled with ice, combine the first three ingredients. Shake and pour into a serving glass. Add ice, soda and garnishes.

Gin Rickey

  1½ oz. (45 mL) gin
  club soda
  lime wedge

Pour gin into a highball glass filled with ice. Add soda and lime wedge.

••
A Rickey can be made with any liquor, soda and lime.
••

Long Island Iced Tea

  1/2 oz. (15 mL) gin
  1/2 oz. (15 mL) vodka
  1/2 oz. (15 mL) rum
  1/2 oz. (15 mL) tequila
  1/2 oz. (15 mL) Triple Sec
  1 oz. (30 mL) bar mix
  cola
  lemon slice

Shake first six ingredients with ice and pour into a Collins or highball glass. Add cola and garnish with lemon. Can also be strained and served without ice.

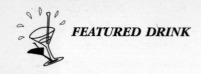

Martini

2 oz. (60 mL) gin
dash of extra dry vermouth

Stir or shake gin and vermouth with ice. Strain straight up into a cocktail glass (though some prefer it over ice). Garnish with an olive or two or three, or a lemon twist.

Martini Madness

There are very few other cocktails as surrounded in myth and mystique. How and when did the martini originate? There are several stories to choose from.

The martini is largely a twentieth-century made-in-America phenomenon, though it probably existed in some form before the turn of the century. Here are a few of the sources credited, any of which could be true:

- In the late 1880s a famous bartender in San Francisco, Jerry Thomas, was told the recipe by a magnanimous stranger on his way to Martinez, California.

- This same Jerry Thomas created the mixture for a stranger who was anticipating a trip to Martinez.

- A Martinez bartender created the cocktail for a celebrating gold miner. The miner wanted champagne but the bar was out, making necessity the mother of Martini invention.

- Some think it may have been named after a rifle, the Martini and Henry, since both the drink and the rifle are known for their "kick."

- Perhaps it was named after Martini and Rossi vermouth, and was the result of a clever marketing scheme.

- Possibly it was invented during the battle of Little Big Horn by Sergeant Martinez, who had been reassigned away from the battle and had time on his hands.

The *Modern Bartender's Guide*, by O. H. Byron (1884), lists a **Martinez** as a variation of the Manhattan, substituting gin for rye whisky. As late as 1927, in *How to Mix Drinks and Serve*, by Paul E. Lowe, this was still the case. In addition, however, there is also a **Martini Cocktail** listed with the following ingredients: 3 dashes Angostura bitters, 6 dashes orange bitters, 1/2 jigger Old Tom gin, 1/2 jigger vermouth. This would have been quite a sweet rendition.

Regardless of its genesis, prohibition served to popularize gin drinks. Here was a liquor that was relatively easy to make, with no aging or special equipment required. Possibly, too, the need in those times to drink covertly and cover up the evidence quickly led to a shrinking of the list of ingredients required. Hence, the minimalist two ingredient martini that we serve today.

The trend towards a drier martini started early. In 1912, Martini di Arma di Taggia claimed to have invented the dry martini for John D. Rockefeller at the Knickerbocker Club in New York. Incidentally, this is yet another theory as to how a variation on a Manhattan became a martini. "Let's get out of these wet clothes and into a dry martini," was apparently uttered by actor Robert Benchley, probably in the 1920s. Sir Winston Churchill was of the opinion that a perfect martini was best built pouring gin into a mixing glass while looking at the vermouth. His sentiments were re-expressed in the movie *Written on the Wind*. One character explains to two others, "The secret is not to pour the vermouth, just to pretend you're pouring it". There was even a **Martini Spike**, really a syringe, manufactured to allow only a drop or two of vermouth to be dispensed.

While one group of politicians, actors, playwrights and man-ufacturers influenced our pursuit of the perfectly pared-down martini, another equally illustrious group sought to introduce a huge variety of ingredients and deviations. President Franklin Roosevelt was a martini maven, yet he frequently experimented with alternate additions. Notably, he served Stalin **Dirty Martinis**, which consisted of gin, vermouth and a dash of the olive brine.

"Shaken, not stirred" aside, Ian Fleming created quite a stir when he penned James Bond as a vodka martini lover. In the 1950s a martini recipe contest garnered well over 200 different suggested additions, including garlic, Pernod, any fruit juice, candy cane and a wild array of garnishes.

So what's in a martini today? What do you think should be in it? Enjoy.

MARTINIS A TO Z

Here are just a few of the possibilities:

Apricot Martini

1/2 oz. (15 mL) vodka
1/2 oz. (15 mL) apricot brandy
1/2 oz. (15 mL) chocolate liqueur (Godiva)
cherry

Combine liquids with ice and shake until well chilled. Serve in a cocktail glass with a cherry.

Blues Martini

1/2 oz. (15 mL) vodka
1/2 oz. (15 mL) gin
dash blue Curaçao

Combine with ice and stir. Strain into a cocktail glass, or serve over ice.

Cajun Martini

3 oz. (90 mL) vodka
dash dry vermouth
1 thin slice garlic
pickled jalapeño pepper slices
cocktail onions

Well in advance, mix the vodka with the garlic and jalapêno and store in a closed container in the freezer. To serve, combine the vodka mixture with vermouth in a mixing glass filled with ice. Strain into a cocktail glass and garnish with onion.

Damn the Weather

1 oz. (30 mL) gin
1/2 oz. (15 mL) Italian vermouth
1/2 oz. (15 mL) orange juice
a few dashes of Cointreau or Triple Sec

Combine all the ingredients with ice and strain into a cocktail glass.

Hawaiian Martini

1/2 oz. (15 mL) gin
1/2 oz. (15 mL) dry vermouth
1/2 oz. (15 mL) sweet vermouth
dash of pineapple juice

Shake with ice and strain into a chilled cocktail glass.

Lemontini

2 oz. (60 mL) lemon vodka
1/2 oz. (15 mL) dry vermouth
dash Cointreau

Swirl Cointreau around in a cocktail glass and discard the excess. Stir vodka and vermouth over ice and strain into prepared cocktail glass.

Mexican Martini

1½ oz. (45 mL) tequila
1 tbsp. (15 mL) dry vermouth
2-3 drops vanilla extract

Shake with ice and strain into a chilled cocktail glass.

Pear Martini

1 oz. (30 mL) vodka
1/2 oz. (15 mL) pear liqueur
pear half

Stir first 2 ingredients with ice and strain into a cocktail glass. Garnish with pear.

Sakitini

2 oz. (60 mL) gin
1/4 oz. (8 mL) sake
olive

Shake gin and sake with ice. Strain into a chilled cocktail glass and garnish with olive. Can also be made with vodka, instead of gin, and a lemon twist.

Vesper Martini

1½ oz. (45 mL) gin
1/2 oz. (15 mL) vodka
dash Kina Lillet

Shake with ice, strain into a cocktail glass and garnish with a lemon slice.

(This is James Bond's other favorite drink.)

Zorbatini

1½ oz. (45 mL) vodka
1/4 oz. (8 mL) Ouzo

Stir with ice and strain. A green olive could garnish.

Negroni

 2 oz. (60 mL) gin
 1/2 oz. (15 mL) sweet vermouth
 3/4 oz. (22 mL) Campari
 orange peel
 splash soda (optional)

Stir gin, vermouth and Campari with ice and strain into a chilled cocktail or rocks glass. Some like this with a splash of soda; some prefer it on the rocks. A few modern versions suggest dry vermouth, although given the bitter taste of Campari, this would not please all.

••

This concoction is named after Count Camillo Negroni. Apparently this Florentine aristocrat requested this combination so frequently during the 1920s, and in more than a few places throughout Italy, that the drink eventually was named in his honor.

••

Pink Gin

 1¾ oz. (50 mL) gin
 dash Angostura bitters

Swirl the bitters around the inside of a chilled cocktail glass to coat. Add gin.

••

Pink Gin was popularized by the British Navy in its endless search for a remedy for the vast array of stomach complaints suffered by its sailors.

••

Pink Lady

 1½ oz. (45 mL) gin
 1 tsp. (5 mL) grenadine
 1/2 tsp. (2.5 mL) cherry brandy
 1/2 oz. (15 mL) cream
 1 egg white

Combine all of the ingredients in a shaker with ice. Shake vigorously and strain into a cocktail glass. To omit the egg white, increase the cream to 1½ oz. (45 mL).

Singapore Sling

1½ oz. (45 mL) gin
2½ oz. (75 mL) bar mix
1/2 oz. (15 mL) grenadine
club soda
1 dash cherry brandy
orange slice
maraschino cherry

In a mixing glass filled with ice combine gin, bar mix and grenadine. Shake well and strain into a Collins glass filled with ice. Add soda to the top and gently stir in dash of cherry brandy. Garnish with fruit. Those paper party parasols are appropriate here too.

••

There are several variations on the Singapore Sling story. Apparently the original, invented by bartender Ngiam Tong Boon at the Raffles Hotel, Singapore in 1915 contained equal parts gin, Bénédictine, cherry brandy and some club soda.

••

Tom Collins

2 oz. (60 mL) gin
1½ oz. (45 mL) lemon juice
1 oz. (30 mL) sugar syrup (or to taste)
club soda
maraschino cherry

Mix gin, lemon juice and sugar syrup in a Collins glass with ice. Top up with soda and garnish with cherry.

••

The sugar syrup is added today because the original Collins was made with Old Tom gin, the sweet gin that is not readily available now.

••

- *Most memorable movie moment about gin:*
  "Of all the gin joints in all the towns in the world, she walks into mine."

  – *Humphrey Bogart,* Casablanca

- *World's best selling gin:*
  Gordon's Gin – more than 65 million bottles are sold per year

- *Literary quote:*
  "You may talk of o'gin an beer
  When you're quartered safe out'ere, . . ."

  – *Rudyard Kipling,* Gunga Din

  A **Gunga Din Martini** combines 1½ oz. (45 mL) gin, 1/2 oz. (15 mL) dry vermouth and the juice of 1/4 orange shaken with ice, strained and garnished with a pineapple slice.

- *Naughty name award:*
  There are several contenders here, yet one submission from San Francisco stands out – **Bitch on Wheels:** 1 oz. (30 mL) gin, 1/4 oz. (8 mL) extra dry vermouth, 1/4 oz. (8 mL) Pernod, 1/4 oz. (8 mL) white crème de menthe. Shake with ice and strain into a chilled cocktail glass.

- *Most royal gin drink name:*
  Queen Elizabeth: Stir 1½ oz. (45 mL) gin, 1/2 oz. (15 mL) Cointreau, 1/2 oz. (15 mL) lemon juice and 1 tsp. (5 mL) Pernod with ice and strain into a chilled cocktail glass.

CHAPTER FIVE

Rum

The word *rum* conjures up a diverse, almost contradictory array of images. On the one hand, there is the tranquil, tropical idyll associated with cocktails such as Daiquiris and Mai Tais. On the other hand, there is the less savory image of demon rum and the slave trade. There is another side too, the swashbuckling, romantic aura of pirates, buccaneers and rum-runners.

RUM SAVVY: HISTORY, PRODUCTION AND STORAGE

Rum is definitely an Islands drink, produced throughout the Caribbean and most of Central America. Puerto Rican rums are the most in demand today.

The presence of rum, as we think of it today, was first reported in records in Barbados around 1650. There is, though, substantial evidence that points to the existence of something similar to rum in ancient times, possibly as far back as 2,000 years ago. Certainly sugarcane grows naturally in other parts of the world, and it is known that Alexander the Great transported sugarcane from China to Egypt. The Moors planted sugarcane throughout Europe and made a rum-like drink by distilling sugarcane.

It was in the Caribbean, however, that sugarcane grew like a weed and became an extremely valuable commodity. From a practical point of view, rum provided traders with an ideal way to store their sugar cane. Distilled, it could not deteriorate with age.

Considering that rum is made from sugarcane, it is interesting to note that sugar is not native to the Caribbean, but, rather, was brought by Christopher Columbus on his second voyage there in 1493.

Barely 50 years after the recorded existence of this new beverage, the British Navy made rum part of its sailors' official rations, and it remained so for almost 300 years, until the practice was discontinued in 1970.

Although the origin of the word *rum* is not known, it seems likely that its association with the English had something to do with it. Rum is a word used as an adjective in certain parts of England to describe something of a good sort. Compared to the rest of a ship's stores, this liquid must have seemed *rum*. In another part of Britain, the word rum was synonymous with disruption. Perhaps rum refers to the physical results of overdrinking it, or to the social tumult resulting from its trade and prevalence. (Temperance zealots pushed the latter derivation.) Less romantic an explanation is the fact that the Latin word for sugar is *saccharum*.

The British Navy is credited with creating the first rum cocktail. Admiral Edward Vernon popularized the notion of mixing the rum ration with water. His reasoning probably included stretching rations and preventing drunkenness. The mixture became known as *grog*, the admiral's nickname due to the grogane cape he often wore. Apparently the infamous buccaneer Henry Morgan took grog one step further and added lime juice in an effort to combat scurvy.

Rum was quickly embraced by the American colonies and it was the first spirit to be distilled in North America. By the end of the seventeenth century, rum was America's most consumed liquor. One early innovation, credited to Benjamin Franklin, was the Rum Flip. Still popular today, a Flip combined rum and beer (probably because it was safer than water), with eggs, cream and spices.

As is the case with liquor in general, neither war nor prohibition ever did much to slow down either the production or consumption of rum; in fact, several rum concoctions trace their origins to those times.

Production Rum is the product of sugarcane. The cane is pressed and the resulting juice is boiled down, clarified, crystallized and separated into sugar and molasses. It is the molasses that is reboiled, then mixed with yeast to ferment it. Each rum manufacturer has its own special strain of yeast, a carefully guarded part of the recipe.

The fermented portion is distilled in continuous column stills that can be more than four storeys tall. This crude rum is then aged. Often it is aged in white oak barrels. If dark rum is desired, the rum is aged in charred barrels, though caramel and assorted other ingredients will still be necessary to achieve the desired color. To create colorless rum, the aging process can be done in stainless steel.

At some point in the aging process, anywhere between one and 10 years, various rums are blended to achieve the right quality. This combining process is the work of a master blender. Again, each manufacturer closely guards its own distinct combinations, considering each a not-so-minor work of art.

Rum flavors vary widely. Generally, most rum from Puerto Rico is dry and light. By law, rums made in Puerto Rico must be aged for one year. The white rums must, therefore, go through a special refiltering process to remove all color. Amber or golden rums have usually been aged about three years. Rums from Jamaica and Demerara tend to be dark and sweet. The Demerara rum, which has a very high alcohol content at around 150-proof, is the type recommended for the infamous **Zombie** cocktail. Barbados rums tend to to golden or dark.

The gold or dark rums are the ones that some people like to sip straight up or on the rocks. Ernest Hemingway, known to love Daiquiris, apparently also proclaimed that sipping rum from a snifter was "the perfect antidote for a rainy day."

Not getting older but getting . . .

At the Barrilito distillery in Puerto Rico, there is a barrel of rum that has been set aside since 1942. It is to be opened and shared throughout San Juan on the day Puerto Rico wins its independence from the United States.

Storage Unopened rum should last indefinitely. Opened, it should be fine for two to three years, especially if kept in a dark, dry, relatively cool place. If rum is a summer drink favorite among your compatriots, keeping it in the fridge may enhance its taste in mixed drinks.

RUM CLASSICS

Many recipes for rum drinks indicate a certain type of rum, although most bartenders feel free to experiment. Ideally, we should all be able to afford the most expensive premium brands going; realistically, you know what works for you.

Bacardi

1½ oz. (45 mL) Bacardi light rum
juice of 1/2 lime
1/2 tsp. (2.5 mL) grenadine

Shake all ingredients well with ice and strain into a cocktail glass.

Boston Sidecar

3/4 oz. (22 mL) light rum
3/4 oz. (22 mL) brandy
3/4 oz. (22 mL) Cointreau
juice of 1/2 lime

Combine in a shaker with ice. Shake well and strain into a cocktail glass.

Cuba Libre

1½ oz. (45 mL) rum
cola
juice of 1/2 lime

Pour rum and lime juice in a highball glass filled with ice. Top up with cola and garnish with a lime wedge.

Legend has it that an American Army lieutenant first experimented with the Cuba Libre combination in Havana in 1898. The Spanish-American war was just over, Cuba was freed and Coca-Cola was the latest thing. Particularly popular during World War II, the somewhat streamlined, de-limed rum and Coke became practically an institution.

Hummer

    1 oz. (30 mL) rum
    1 oz. (30 mL) coffee liqueur such as Kahlúa
    2 scoops vanilla ice cream

Mix all ingredients together in a food processor or blender. Pour into a large stemmed or rocks glass.

 **FEATURED DRINK**

Daiquiri

    1½ oz. (45 mL) light rum
    1/2 tsp. (2.5 mL) sugar syrup
    juice of 1/2 lime

Shake all ingredients with ice and strain into a cocktail glass. Could be garnished with a lime or orange slice.

There are several variations of this drink; one simple approach is to replace the light rum with dark rum.

Prescription Daiquiri

Close in time and place to the Cuba Libre,
this libation was also conceived in 1898, in
the small town of Daiquiri, Cuba. There was
an outbreak of malaria and the only medicine available to
the town's doctors was rum. American engineers working
nearby suggested the addition of lime and sugar to help the
medicine go down. Soon, all the locals, sick or not, were
enjoying this tonic. Its reputation soon spread and Daiquiris
became a favorite with influential figures such as Ernest
Hemingway and F. Scott Fitzgerald. In fact, the first official
printed mention of a Daiquiri was in Fitzgerald's 1920 novel,
This Side of Paradise.

DAIQUIRI VARIATIONS

There are numerous Daiquiri mix kits, even premixed selections, available at your grocery store or at the liquor store. Certainly
convenient, you might want to try one or two and taste-test the
results.

Banana Daiquiri

1½ oz. (45 mL) light rum
1/2 oz. (15 mL) lime juice
1 tsp. (5 mL) crème de banane, or sugar syrup
1/2 soft banana, sliced

Combine ingredients with 1/2 cup (125 mL) of cracked ice in
blender. Pulse until smooth and pour into a chilled stemmed glass.

••

Due to their sugar content, any appropriately flavored liqueurs can replace
sugar syrup.

••

Strawberry Daiquiri

1½ oz. (45 mL) rum
1/2 oz. (15 mL) Cointreau or Triple Sec
1 oz. (30 mL) lime juice
1/2 cup (125 mL) very ripe strawberries
1/2 tsp. (2.5 mL) superfine sugar, or to taste
1 cup (250 mL) crushed ice

Combine all ingredients in a blender and pour into a large stemmed glass. Garnish with a strawberry.

Mai Tai

1 oz. (30 mL) Jamaican rum
1 oz. (30 mL) Martinique rum
1/2 oz. (15 mL) Curaçao
1/4 oz. (8 mL) rock-candy syrup
1/4 oz. (8 mL) Orgeat syrup
lime twist
mint sprig
pineapple spear

Vigorously shake all the liquid ingredients with ice. Pour into a chilled highball or Collins glass and garnish. (Orgeat is an almond-flavored syrup.)

••

Though variations of the Mai Tai abound, this version is apparently the original as built by Vic Bergeron, of Trader Vic's fame, in 1944. He presented this concoction to two friends from Tahiti. One of the two, Mrs. Carrie Wright, exclaimed, "Mai Tai . . . roe ae!", Tahitian for "Out of this world . . . the best."

Bergeron himself promoted this drink everywhere, even through various shipping and hotel lines. Still the story of its origin became confused, so in frustration, in 1970 Bergeron extracted a sworn statement from Mrs. Wright to certify his creation of the Mai Tai.

••

Piña Colada

2 oz. (60 mL) light rum
1 oz. (30 mL) coconut cream
1 oz. (30 mL) whipping cream
6 oz. (180 mL) fresh pineapple juice
1/2 cup (125 mL) crushed ice
maraschino cherry
orange slice
pineapple spear

In a blender, combine the first 5 ingredients. Blend until smooth then pour into a Collins or highball glass and garnish with fruit.

••

Probably one of the most popular of tropical rum drinks, the Piña Colada definitely comes from San Juan, Puerto Rico, but two creators lay claim to it. In 1978, the Piña Colada was celebrated in a popular hit song, Rupert Holmes' *Escape (The Piña Colada Song)*.

••

Planter's Punch

2 oz. (60 mL) dark rum
3 oz. (90 mL) orange juice
1 tsp. (5 mL) sugar
juice of 1/2 lemon, or 1/2 lime
dash grenadine
maraschino cherry
orange slice

Vigorously shake the sugar and liquid ingredients in a shaker with cracked ice. Pour into a chilled Collins glass and garnish with fruit. Some bartenders like to add club soda to this.

••

The Myers's Rum distillery in Jamaica lays claim to this drink. Apparently Planter's Punch was created and served in 1879 to celebrate the founding of this company. The original recipe did not include club soda. Check page 115 for a crowd-sized Planter's Punch.

••

Zombie

2 oz. (60 mL) light rum
1 oz. (30 mL) dark rum
1/2 oz. (15 mL) Demerara rum (150-proof)
1 oz. (30 mL) Curaçao
1 tsp. (5 mL) Pernod
1 oz. (30 mL) lemon juice
1 oz. (30 mL) orange juice
1 oz. (30 mL) pineapple juice
1/2 oz. (15 mL) papaya juice
1/4 oz. (8 mL) grenadine
1/2 oz. (15 mL) Orgeat syrup
mint sprig
pineapple spear

Combine all liquids in a blender with 3/4 cup (190 mL) of cracked ice. Blend until smooth. Pour into a chilled Collins glass and garnish with mint and pineapple. If desired, reserve the 150-proof rum and float it on top of the cocktail with a sprinkle of powdered sugar.

••

A big drink requiring the ingredients of a fairly well-stocked bar, the Zombie first appeared around 1939 and was popularized in tropical theme bars that were prevalent in the '40s, '50s and '60s. Even now, the Zombie is a popular choice among young drinkers.

••

Further rum renditions There are several other rum drink recipes out there and surely some have not yet been thought of. Rum is versatile and can be used in recipes usually calling for other liquors. It is also found in drink recipes such as **Long Island Iced Tea**, on page 35.

Rum Collins

2 oz. (60 mL) rum
1 tsp. (5 mL) superfine sugar
1 oz. (30 mL) lime juice
club soda
lime or orange wheel
maraschino cherry

In a Collins glass filled with ice, combine rum, sugar and lime juice. Stir well and top up with soda. Garnish with fruit. **Hint:** the sugar will dissolve more readily if you stir it with the lime juice first.

Rum Sour

2 oz. (60 mL) rum
1 oz. (30 mL) lemon juice
1/2 tsp. (2.5 mL) superfine sugar
orange wheel
maraschino cherry

In a shaker glass filled with ice, combine rum, lemon juice and sugar. Shake well and stain into a cocktail or sour glass. Garnish.

Rum Martini

2 oz. (60 mL) light rum
1/2 oz. (15 mL) dry vermouth
lemon twist or olive

Mix rum and vermouth with ice. Stir well and strain it into a cocktail glass. Garnish.

Pancho Villa

1 oz. (30 mL) light rum
1 oz. (30 mL) gin
1/2 oz. (15 mL) apricot brandy
1 tsp. (5 mL) cherry brandy
1 tsp. (5 mL) pineapple juice

Mix all ingredients with ice in a shaker or blender. Strain into a chilled cocktail or rocks glass with ice.

Tiger's Milk

1½ oz. (45 mL) amber rum
1½ oz. (45 mL) cognac
4–6 oz. (120-180 mL) 10% cream or milk
sugar syrup to taste
grated nutmeg or cinnamon

Place first four ingredients in a shaker filed with cracked ice. Shake well and pour into a chilled wine glass. Sprinkle with nutmeg or cinnamon. This may also be made in a blender.

FYI

- *Most popular sing-along rum song:*

  Rum and Coca-Cola, *popularized by the Andrews Sisters during World War II*

- *Most memorable movie moment:*
  "Why didn't you tell me it's a Rum and Coke?"

  - Tom Cruise in Cocktail, *(1988) in frustration at not realizing that a Cuba Libre is basically a Rum and Coke with lime juice*

- *World's best-selling rum:*
  Bacardi, now of Puerto Rico, originally from Cuba (This is not just the best-selling rum, it is the best-selling liquor in the world.)

- *Literary references to rum:*
  "There's nought, no doubt, so much the spirit calms
     As rum and true religion."

  - Don Juan, by Lord Byron

  "Fifteen men on the dead man's chest
     Yo ho ho, and a bottle of rum!"

  - Treasure Island, by Robert Louis Stevenson

In a buccaneer mood? Try a **Jolly Roger:** Shake 1 oz. (30 mL) rum, 1 oz. (30 mL) banana liqueur and 2 oz. (60 mL) lemon juice with ice. Pour into a chilled wine glass.

- *Naughty name award:*
  Between the Sheets: Combine 3/4 oz. (22 mL) light rum, 3/4 oz. (22 mL) brandy, 3/4 oz. (22 mL) Cointreau, 1½ oz. (45 mL) lemon juice and 1/2 cup (125 mL) cracked ice in a shaker or blender. Strain into a chilled cocktail glass.

- *Will that be cash or rum?*
  Apparently the builders of the first hospital in Sydney, Australia were paid 450,000 gallons (1,800,000 L) of rum instead of cash.

- *Famous-name rum drinks:*
  Rum seems to have ingratiated itself all over the place, especially among writers, artists and performers. Consider the **Gaugin**, the **Hemingway**, and the **Mary Pickford**.

  Gaugin: In a blender combine 2 oz. (60 mL) light rum with 1 tsp. (5 mL) each of passion fruit syrup, lime juice, lemon juice, and 1/2 cup (125 mL) of crushed ice. Blend until smooth and pour into a chilled rocks glass. Garnish with a twist of lime.

  Hemingway: According to the Bacardi bunch, Hemingway would have loved this. Certainly he was very fond of rum and fruit juice combinations. Mix 1½ oz. (45 mL) light rum with the juice of 1/2 lime, 1/4 oz. (8 mL) grapefruit juice, 1/4 oz. (8 mL) maraschino liqueur and ice. Serve with ice.

  Mary Pickford: This Canadian-born queen of the silent screen either requested or inspired this combination. Mix 1½ oz. (45 mL) of rum, 1½ oz. (45 mL) pineapple juice, a splash each of grenadine and maraschino liqueur with ice. Can be strained or served with ice.

CHAPTER SIX

Vodka

The only alcoholic beverage that won't freeze in Winnipeg, vodka is best known for what it doesn't do. Refusing to freeze, vodka also has no color, no odor and, with the exception of flavored varieties, no discernible taste. It is these negative descriptions that makes vodka what it is today: one of the most popular spirits in North America. With flavorful additions, vodka is the perfect underpinning for a vast array of very tasty cocktails.

VODKA SAVVY: HISTORY, PRODUCTION AND STORAGE

Both Russia and Poland take credit for vodka's creation. The word *vodka* is a diminutive form of the Russian word for water, *voda*. So vodka means *little water*.

Vodka is mentioned in Russian literature as early as the twelfth century, though it is thought that the word might have then referred to any alcoholic spirit. Like gin, and so many other alcoholic beverages, it seems vodka started life as a medicinal tonic, a prescription for gout, gallstones and stomach ailments. Its charcoal-filtering technique was discovered by a Russian pharmaceutical chemist around 1810.

Vodka has always been extremely popular in Russia – perhaps too popular. At one time there were more than 4,000 brands of vodka for sale inside Russia. Vodka production was banned in the Soviet Union from 1914 until 1925, when it was resumed, ostensibly for medicinal purposes, with the state in control of the industry.

The popularity of vodka in North America is a relatively recent phenomenon. Its initial presence here was thanks to the Smirnoff family, who fled to the United States during the Russian revolution. Their small vodka distillery, and an ingenious advertising campaign in the 1940s, created a demand that remains strong even today.

Even in the 1980s, when liquor sales generally were declining, vodka sales increased. Aside from the fact that it is a great mixer, there have been some spectacularly successful marketing campaigns that have created the vodka image: clear, clean and youthful.

Production Contrary to popular belief, vodka is not necessarily made from potatoes. It may have once come from potatoes, though just as likely from any other vegetable source, grain or cane – whatever product had the biggest surplus.

In Turkey, vodka may be made from beets, while Britain tends to produce vodka from molasses. Today most of the best vodkas are made from grains.

The base material is fermented into a mash. This is then distilled to a very high proof, 190-proof or higher. Some high-end vodkas may be triple-distilled. The result is a very pure spirit that is then slowly passed through a vegetable charcoal or activated carbon filter. The filtering process is so crucial that some distillers patent certain types. Some vodkas may even be filtered through fine quartz sand. This process creates a liquor free of flavor, aroma or color. Usually it is not aged, though Stárka, or gold vodka, has been aged for about 10 years.

Flavored vodkas, of which there are several to choose from, are made by later adding natural flavoring materials. (Somewhat ironically, there are literally dozens of flavors.) The most popular include citrus, black currant, cranberry, peppers of all kinds, honey and raspberry. One type from Poland is made by infusing zubrowka grass. It is sold with a single long blade of grass floating in the bottle.

Storage Ideally, vodka should be stored in the refrigerator or freezer, especially if it is a premium brand and to be imbibed straight. Although vodka is supposedly tasteless, each brand does have its own character, so a top-quality (expensive) vodka would be recommended if the vodka will be on its own or dominant, as in a vodka martini. Otherwise, for flavorful cocktails, any name brand should be fine. An open bottle of vodka should have a shelf life of about three years so long as it is stored in a cool, dry place.

VODKA CLASSICS

Feel free to experiment. Vodka lends itself to almost any flavoring.

Alexander Nevsky

1 oz. (30 mL) vodka
1 oz. (30 mL) apricot liqueur
1/2 oz. (15 mL) lemon juice
4 oz. (120 mL) orange juice
orange wheel slice

Combine all the liquids in a shaker or blender with cracked ice. Mix well. Pour into a chilled wine glass and garnish with orange slice.

••

Alexander Nevsky was made a saint by the Eastern Orthodox Church for stopping an invasion of Germans and Swedes into Russia. Likely, the cocktail was created in America though, since traditionally Russians prefer to drink their vodka straight.

••

Black Russian

1½ oz. (45 mL) vodka
3/4 oz. (22 mL) Kahlúa

Shake vigorously with cracked ice and pour into a chilled old-fashioned glass.

••

A variation of this cocktail, **Black Magic**, calls for the addition of a few dashes of lemon juice and a lemon twist to the above ingredients.

••

Bloody Caesar

1½ oz. (45 mL) vodka
6 oz. (180 mL) Clamato juice
dash or two of Worcestershire sauce
dash Tabasco sauce

salt and pepper (to taste)
lime wedge
celery stalk
celery salt

Rim a highball glass with lime and dip the rim in a celery salt-coarse salt mixture. Fill glass with ice cubes, pour in liquids, season and stir gently. Garnish with celery stalk and lime.

••

One of Canada's most popular cocktails, it is virtually unknown elsewhere in the world. Credit for its creation goes to Walter Chell, who designed this concoction to mark the opening of a restaurant in Calgary in the late 1960s.

••

 FEATURED DRINK

Bloody Mary

2 oz. (60 mL) vodka
4-6 oz. (120-180 mL) tomato juice
1 tsp. (5 mL) lemon juice
dash Worcestershire sauce
dash Tabasco sauce
pepper
celery salt or salt
1/2 tsp. (2.5 mL) dill (dried or fresh)
celery stalk
lime wedge

Reserve the lime wedge and celery stalk for garnish. Combine all the other ingredients in a shaker with cracked ice. Shake gently or the tomato juice will separate. Strain into a Collins or highball glass filled with ice.

Bloody Mary – lore and more

There are numerous stories regarding the origins of the Bloody Mary and its optimum ingredients. Most agree that the basic tomato juice-vodka combination has been around for quite a while, probably first put forward in the 1920s by Fernand Petiot, a bartender at Harry's New York Bar in Paris. It is known that when Petiot moved to New York and started bartending at the luxurious St. Regis Hotel, he brought the Bloody Mary recipe with him. Management thought the name too vulgar, so for a time it was renamed the **Red Snapper**.

Where did the name Bloody Mary come from? Some suggest that it is after the infamous daughter of King Henry VIII, Mary, who, when she became queen, sent hundreds of Protestants to their bloody death. Others think Mary may have been a bartender's girlfriend.

Over time, the Bloody Mary has evolved. Originally it was not a tall drink, but meant to be served in a cocktail glass. Perhaps as a result of its larger size, many are encouraged to experiment with the spices. Some swear by the addition of horseradish; others add A-1, basil, oregano, garlic, soy sauce, anchovy paste or capers. There are also several packaged Bloody Mary mixes, if you don't like guess work.

What is the significance of the celery stalk? Celery is thought by some to relieve blood pressure problems. It is interesting to note how many drinks or their component parts are thought to be remedies and, if nothing else, a Bloody Mary is thought to be a remedy for a hangover. Celery is also involved in medieval love potions. Perhaps the original cocktail was meant for a girlfriend after all. In Roman times celery was used in funeral wreaths, so maybe the connection to a vengeful queen is apt.

Bull Shot

1½ oz. (45 mL) vodka
4 oz. (120 mL) cold beef bouillon
1 tsp. (5 mL) lemon juice
dash Worcestershire sauce
dash Tabasco sauce
salt and pepper (to taste)
1/2 tsp. (2.5 mL) horseradish (optional)
lemon wedge

Combine the first seven ingredients in a shaker with ice. Shake well and strain into a double rocks or highball glass filled with ice. Garnish with lemon wedge.

Like the Bloody Mary, the Bull Shot is suggested as a hangover remedy.

Cape Codder

1½ oz. (45 mL) vodka
4-5 oz. (120-150 mL) cranberry juice
1 tsp. (5 mL) sugar syrup – optional
dash lime juice
lime wedge

Reserve the lime wedge for garnish. Shake vodka, cranberry juice, sugar syrup and lime juice with cracked ice. Pour into a chilled double rocks or highball glass and garnish.

Cossack Charge

1½ oz. (45 mL) vodka
1/2 oz. (15 mL) cognac
1/2 oz. (15 mL) cherry brandy

Mix all with cracked ice in a shaker or blender and pour into a chilled cocktail glass.

Harvey Wallbanger

1½ oz. (45 mL) vodka
4 oz. (120 mL) orange juice
1/2 oz. (15 mL) Galliano

Pour vodka and orange juice into a chilled Collins glass about one-third full of ice. Stir, then float the Galliano on top.

....

Harvey was a surfer dude created for a marketing campaign by Galliano. Doubtless the campaign helped enhance vodka's youth appeal.

....

Moscow Mule

1½ oz. (45 mL) vodka
1 oz. (30 mL) lime juice
4 oz. (120 mL) ginger beer
lime wedge

Pour vodka and lime juice into a chilled mug about one-third filled with ice. Top up with ginger beer and garnish with lime.

....

This is the drink that is thought to have propelled vodka into the mainstream. The Smirnoff company used this recipe in an extremely successful marketing campaign in the 1940s. Originally the drink was promoted with copper mugs, each inscribed with the likeness of a mule. The mugs became collector's items. Smirnoff became the most widely selling vodka in the world.

....

Screwdriver

1½ oz. (45 mL) vodka
4 oz. (120 mL) orange juice
orange slice

Into a chilled highball or double rocks glass, filled one-third with ice, pour vodka, then orange juice. Stir and garnish. Tastes best with freshly squeezed orange juice.

St. Petersburg

2 oz. (60 mL) vodka
1/4 tsp. (1.25 mL) orange bitters
orange wedge or twist

Sir the vodka and bitters with ice and strain into a chilled cocktail
or old-fashioned glass. Drop wedge or peel into the drink.

White Russian

1½ oz. (45 mL) vodka
1 oz. (30 mL) Kahlúa
1 oz. (30 mL) cream

Vigorously shake all of the ingredients with ice. Strain into a chilled
cocktail glass or an old-fashioned glass filled with ice. White crème
de cacao can be substituted for the Kahlúa.

Vodka and . . .

Vodka goes with, and enhances, so many other flavors that it
easily substitutes for other liquors, and has been subject to quite a
few interesting couplings.

Vodka Martini

2-3 oz. (60-90 mL) vodka
dash dry vermouth
olive or lemon twist

Stir the vodka and vermouth with a lot of ice quickly. Strain into a
chilled cocktail glass and garnish.

Fuzzy Navel

1 oz. (30 mL) vodka
1 oz. (30 mL) peach schnapps
4 oz. (120 mL) orange juice

In a highball glass filed with ice, pour the ingredients in the order
given and stir well.

Mudslide

1 oz. (30 mL) vodka
1 oz. (30 mL) coffee liqueur
1 oz. (30 mL) Irish Cream

Combine all with cracked ice in a shaker or blender and pour into a chilled old-fashioned glass. Mudslides are also available premixed at the liquor store.

Vodka Collins

1-2 oz. (30-60 mL) vodka
2 oz. (60 mL) sour mix
club soda
maraschino cherry
orange slice

Shake vodka and sour mix well with ice. Strain into a Collins glass filled with ice. Top up with soda and garnish.

Vodka Grasshopper

1/2 oz. (15 mL) vodka
3/4 oz. (22 mL) green Crème de Menthe
3/4 oz. (22 mL) white Crème de Cacao

Vigourously shake all the ingredients and strain into a chilled cocktail glass.

Vodka Sour

1½ - 2 oz. (45-60 mL) vodka
3/4 oz. (22 mL) lemon juice
1 tsp. (5 mL) sugar syrup
lemon slice
maraschino cherry

Combine vodka, lemon juice and sugar syrup with cracked ice and shake well. Strain into a chilled sour glass and garnish.

Vodka Tonic

    1½ oz. (45 mL) vodka

    tonic water

    lime wedge

Pour vodka into a highball glass one-third full of ice. Top up with tonic and garnish.

Vodka Shooters

    Shooters are flamboyant concoctions. Characterized by crazy names, creative combinations and a deceptively high alcohol content, they are meant to be downed in one gulp. Often served in a shot glass, or test tube-type glasses sometimes called tooters, shooters have been particularly popular with the young bar crowd. Equally enjoyable at home, feel free to substitute available glassware.

Antifreeze

    1½ oz. (45 mL) vodka

    1/2 oz. (15 mL) Midori

Vigourously shake with ice, strain and pour.

Bubble Gum

    1/2 oz. (15 mL) vodka

    1/2 oz. (15 mL) banana liqueur

    1/2 oz. (15 mL) peach schnapps

    1/2 oz. (15 mL) orange juice

Shake with ice, strain and pour.

Hot Lips

    1½ oz. (45 mL) cranberry vodka

    1/4 oz. (8 mL) Goldschlager

Shake with ice, strain and pour.

Juicy Fruit

Equal parts:
- vodka
- peach schnapps
- Midori
- pineapple juice

Shake with ice, strain and pour. These recipes can be made in batches and divided. For four, combine 1½ oz. (45 mL) of each ingredient.

Screaming Orgasm

Equal parts:
- vodka
- Irish Cream
- Kahlúa
- Amaretto

Combine and pour, as above. See page 102 for a quieter orgasm.

Sex on the Beach

See page 102.

Sweet Tart

- 1 oz. (30 mL) vodka
- 1/4 oz. (8 mL) raspberry liqueur
- 1/4 oz. (8 mL) lime juice
- 1/4 oz. (8 mL) pineapple juice

Shake with ice, strain and pour.

Vodka Tootsie Roll

Equal parts:
- vodka
- Kahlúa
- orange juice

Combine and pour.

- *Most memorable vodka movie moment:*
  Any James Bond movie, as Bond's favorite drink was the vodka Martini, "shaken, not stirred."

- *World's best-selling vodka:*
  Smirnoff made in the United States since about 1930.

- *Amazing advertising campaigns:*
  Aside from Smirnoff's Moscow Mule recipe and their popular, ongoing breathless slogan, the marketing behind Absolut Vodka is also notable. The campaign has been running since the 1980s, and basically highlights the company's vodka bottle in a variety of settings. Considered one of the most successful ad campaigns ever, there is even a book about the campaign.

- *Naughty name award:*
  So many to choose from – **Screaming Orgasm**, **Sex on the Beach** and **Silk Panties** (equal parts vodka and peach schnapps), to name but a few.

CHAPTER SEVEN

Whisky

Most people think of scotch when the word whisky comes up. Certainly Scotch whisky is a prominent product with many diehard devotees, especially concerning single-malt or single-cask malt products. Generally, though, it is accepted that whisky originated in Ireland. It was made for medicinal purposes by monks, at least as far back as the twelfth century. Today it is made around the world – and not just for medicinal reasons.

WHISKY SAVVY: HISTORY, PRODUCTION AND STORAGE

The first written records of whisky in Scotland didn't appear until late in the fifteenth century. Irish monks had brought this liquid gold with them when they set out to convert the Scots to Christianity. Perhaps whisky helped sweeten the concept of religious life. In Ireland and Scotland it was called *uisge beatha*, Gaelic for *water of life*.

The word whisky is thought to have been coined by the English who shortened the Gaelic to their own pronunciation of the first word, so that *uisge* became *whisky*. Inevitably, whisky was spread throughout both the Old World and New. For some reason, Ireland and the United States spell whisk(e)y with an "e"; all other countries leave the "e" out.

Irish whiskey (spelled with an "e") is made from barley and water, like scotch. Irish whiskey is generally somewhat lighter in both color and taste. This is because, in Ireland, the malted grain is usually dried in closed, smokeless kilns so that the smoky, peaty flavor associated with scotch is deliberately absent. Irish whiskey is also the only whisky to be distilled three times.

Towards the end of the eighteenth century there may have been close to 2,000 whisky distilleries in Ireland, most of them "private". Starting with an Act of Parliament in England in 1823, to regulate distilleries and collect taxes, circumstances would see that number dwindle to only a handful today. Nevertheless, Irish whiskey is still appreciated. Most of us are familiar with it, whether we know it or not, as a component of Irish Cream, one of the world's best-selling liqueurs.

Scotch whisky Up until the mid-1800s, much of the scotch produced in Scotland was done so illegally. In 1823 alone, approximately 14,000 illegal stills were uncovered. Imagine how many were not found!

This early scotch was made from barley malt and water, like single-malt scotch is today, but the taste was harsh and strong. The invention of the Coffey still soon changed that. This new type of still, also known as a patent still, produced a lighter, more generally palatable whisky. In addition, other grains besides barley were experimented with. By the 1860s the notion of blending malt barley whisky with other grain whiskies caught on. Apparently this was what the world was waiting for, since today more than 90 percent of whisky made is used in a blended product.

There are two types of Scotch whisky. Malt whisky is made entirely from malt barley. The smoky taste that is so evident in malt whisky comes from peat that is used to fire the kilns that dry the malted barley. When malted barley is combined with unmalted barley and corn, grain whisky is made.

Scotch whisky is aged for a minimum of three years by law, though usually the aging is much longer. Aging of whisky can only take place in the barrel. Though it could be bottled elsewhere, to be called scotch it must have been distilled and aged for at least three years in Scotland.

American whiskey (spelled with an "e") was certainly not the first liquor to be distilled in America, yet ironically, their Whiskey Rebellion, in the early 1790s, required a larger army to put down than had been required to win the War of Independence. In order to avoid taxes that the government intended to levy, many farmers moved on towards Kentucky and Tennessee.

It was in Kentucky that America's best-known whisky was formulated. A Baptist minister, Elijah Craig, is popularly thought of as the creator of the first corn-based whisky, **bourbon**. Craig and other distillers in the area had started to use corn in the late 1700s because it was more plentiful. Craig's most significant contribution to the process, though, was his experiment with aging whisky in charred oak barrels. This style of whisky was quite distinct, and it soon became known by the place where it was from, Bourbon County whiskey, short form – bourbon.

By law, bourbon must be made from at least 51-percent corn, and aged in new, charred oak barrels for at least four years. **Tennessee whiskey** is a relative newcomer in terms of official recognition. In 1941, the American government granted separate status to this whisky. Basically like bourbon, it is different in that it is filtered through sugar-maple charcoal.

Canadian whisky is made from a mix of grains, rye, barley, corn and wheat, and aged for a minimum of three years, though usually aging is for six years. Different types of casks may be used for ageing. They could be new charred oak, or they may have been previously used for sherry, brandy or bourbon.

Canadian whisky is known throughout North America as a high-quality, smooth, light-tasting product. Consumption in the United States has always been steady, and escalated sharply during the American Civil War and Prohibition. There are numerous colorful tales to be uncovered, especially during Prohibition. One such tale places the blame for the 1929 St. Valentine's Day Massacre on the theft of a shipment of Canadian whisky en route to Al Capone. Another story insists that Winston Churchill learned his habit of serving whisky in a silver teapot from a practice during Canada's Prohibition.

Rye Both Canadian whisky and bourbon are often mistakenly thought of as rye. In order to be a rye whisky the product must contain at least 51-percent rye and be matured in new charred oak barrels for a minimum of two years. It will be labelled as such on the bottle. While Canadian whisky likely has rye in it, all Canadian distillers, except for one, make their whisky with more corn than rye. Rye's flavor is distinct, as is the grain it comes from.

Production No matter which whisky you prefer, the methods used to produce it are similar. Grain, some of which is malted, is crushed and boiled with water. Yeast is added. This mixture is distilled, preferably twice (three times in Ireland), then aged in wooden barrels, usually made of oak. Between aging and bottling, blending will most likely occur.

Despite the consistency of this basic process, the final product of each type of whisky, from each distillery, is quite unique. There are several factors that are known to contribute to these unique qualities. The water used is extremely important, as it is a main ingredient in the basic product and necessary for diluting the whisky as it ages and when it is bottled. The wood in which the whisky is aged has an influence, whether it is new, old, charred or flavored. Even the air in which the barrels sit to age is considered crucial since wood breathes. If the whisky is blended, of course, that formula is crucial too. Amongst all the known variables involved with whisky, there are also the unknowns, the mystique that gives whisky a lot of its charm.

Whisky distinctions Part of the mystique surrounding whisky comes from the variety available within each type. Here are some of the distinctions you will be choosing from:

Scotch Whisky
Blended scotch, which is a combination of malt and grain whiskies, still dominates the market internationally. There are three styles of blended scotch. **Standard scotch** generally contains only 20 to 30 percent malt whisky. **Premium** probably has close to 45 percent malt whisky, and is somewhat more expensive than standard scotch. **Deluxe scotch** will have more than 50 percent malt whisky.

Single-malt scotch is a pure malt whisky, though it too is blended. Various strengths and ages of malt whisky from one single distillery are mixed together. The age stated on the bottle is the age of the youngest whisky used.

Single-cask malt scotch is produced and bottled, from one single distillation, no blending. This scotch is very expensive as it is considered a distillery's finest product.

Irish Whiskey

Both pure malt and blended whiskies are produced. Blended whisky is the predominant product, but Irish blended whisky is likely to have a high malt content, possibly up to 80 percent in some products.

American Whiskey

Blended whisky in the United States must contain 20 percent straight whisky, which is combined with neutral spirits and other grains whiskies. **Straight whisky** is made either from one grain, or one grain must comprise at least 51-percent of the mix. Bourbon and Tennessee whisky are both made from at least 51-percent corn.

Canadian Whisky

Since all Canadian whisky is made from a mixture of grains, with no set percentage constraints, it is considered blended. If a brand is labelled **rye**, then it will contain at least 51-percent rye.

Storage Unopened, whisky will last forever since no further aging or maturing goes on in the bottle. Opened, it should be stored in a cool, dry place and it will have a shelf-life of at least two years.

All whiskies can be enjoyed straight or with ice, with water, soda or mixed in one of many cocktail recipes. For drinking unadorned, a premium brand might be recommended, though whisky tastes are highly individual. If you do settle on a brand you like best, be sure to order it when you order in a bar or restaurant, since scotch and soda can mean many different things.

WHISKY CLASSICS

As you will see, whisky is an adaptable liquor. Each recipe will suggest the type of whisky that is recommended, though several variations have been created by substituting one type for another. Bourbon and Tennessee whisky are frequently interchanged. Many people prefer the lighter flavors of a blended whisky, especially Canadian, in mixed drinks.

Blackthorn

1½ oz. (45 mL) Irish whiskey
1½ oz. (45 mL) dry vermouth
a few dashes of Pernod
a few dashes of Angostura bitters

Shake all with cracked ice and pour into a chilled rocks glass.

Boilermaker

1⅓ oz. (40 mL) Irish whiskey
12 oz. (375 mL) beer

The whisky is served in a shot glass, separate from the glass of beer. To drink, the whisky should be consumed in one gulp, then the beer, somewhat more leisurely.

Irish Fix

2 oz. (60 mL) Irish whiskey
1/2 oz. (15 mL) Irish Mist
1 oz. (30 mL) pineapple juice
1/2 oz. (15 mL) lemon juice
1/2 tsp. (2.5 mL) sugar syrup
orange slice
lemon slice

Shake all the liquids with cracked ice. Strain and pour into an old-fashioned glass filled with ice. Garnish with fruit.

Irish Kilt

1 oz. (30 mL) Irish whiskey
1 oz. (30 mL) scotch
1 oz. (30 mL) lemon juice
1½ oz. (45 mL) sugar syrup
dashes of orange bitters

Combine and shake all ingredients with ice. Strain and pour into a chilled cocktail glass.

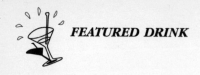

Manhattan

2 oz. (60 mL) blended whisky
splash or so of sweet or dry vermouth
dash Angostura bitters
maraschino cherry

Mix the liquids with ice then strain into a chilled cocktail glass. Garnish with the cherry.

The Manhattan was created in 1874 at the Manhattan Club in New York, for Lady Jenny Churchill, Winston Churchill's mother. The occasion was a banquet, thrown by Lady Churchill in honor of a famous lawyer of the day.

Tastes have changed over time, so it is likely that the original Manhattan contained more than a splash of sweet vermouth. In fact, a recipe published in 1927 calls for equal amounts of whisky and vermouth. One variation today, the **Perfect Manhattan**, calls for 1/8 oz. (4 mL) of both sweet and dry vermouth, garnished with a lemon twist.

And what about that maraschino? It's really nothing more than a good-looking cherry preserved in a strong liqueur. The ideal liqueur is Maraschino itself, a sweet liqueur made from the small, black Dalmation cherry. These days you're more likely to find maraschino cherries preserved in a flavored syrup. Either way, the cherry garnish is essential to give a Manhattan that finishing touch of elegance.

Mint Julep

2-3 oz. (60-90 mL) bourbon
6-15 fresh mint leaves
1/2 oz. (15 mL) sugar syrup
mint sprig

Muddle (mash and stir) the mint leaves with the sugar syrup in the bottom of a silver cup. Stir in some of the bourbon, then fill the glass with crushed ice. Pour in the rest of the bourbon and stir until the cup starts to frost. Place a generous sprig of mint on top. Serve with straws just barely taller than the mint garnish.

Juleps are not a new invention. Webster's 1806 dictionary defined them as a kind of liquid medicine. Today they invoke images of languorous southern summers and, as such, make for a fun frosty drink.

In the United States mint juleps are traditionally enjoyed on the first Saturday in May (if not through the year). This is Kentucky Derby Day, and many a party revolves around both the horse race and the drink.

The great debate that lingers now is whether or not the mint is meant for flavor or fragrance. Some variations of the recipe omit the muddled mint leaves, though the majority include them. Some bars cheat and pour in a drop or two of crème de menthe.

Old-Fashioned

1½ - 2 oz. (45-60 mL) blended whisky
1/2 tsp. (2.5 mL) sugar syrup
2-3 dashes Angostura bitters
splash club soda or water
maraschino cherry
orange slice

In an old-fashioned glass, combine sugar syrup, bitters, soda or water and stir until sugar is dissolved. Add the whisky and ice. Stir thoroughly and garnish with fruit.

••

Story has it that the Old-Fashioned was created for a retired Civil War general in Kentucky. The general didn't much like the taste of whisky, so this recipe was meant to tempt him.

As the point is to sweeten the whisky, variations abound. One alternative suggests mashing the maraschino cherry, without the stem, into the sugar syrup and bitters. Other variations include using a sugar cube or even honey.

••

Paddy Cocktail

1½ oz. (45 mL) Irish whiskey
3/4 oz. (22 mL) sweet vermouth
a few dashes of Angostura bitters

Combine and shake all the ingredients with cracked ice. Pour into a chilled cocktail glass.

Rob Roy

2 oz. (60 mL) scotch
1/2 oz. (15 mL) sweet vermouth
maraschino cherry

Stir scotch and vermouth with plenty of ice. Strain into a chilled cocktail glass and garnish with cherry.

The Rob Roy is named after a Scottish hero-outlaw who was forever immortalized by Sir Walter Scott's novel of the same name. Basically a Rob Roy is like a Manhattan, is like a Paddy Cocktail, and is not too different from an Old-Fashioned. All are variations on a theme.

Rusty Nail

1½ oz. (45 mL) scotch
1 oz. (30 mL) Drambuie

In a chilled old-fashioned glass filled with ice, stir the scotch and Drambuie together. Some bartenders prefer to float the Drambuie on the scotch, no stirring. Others prefer this cocktail neat, in which case it is strained into a cocktail glass. Still others prefer equal parts scotch and Drambuie.

Sazerac

2 oz. (60 mL) bourbon
1 sugar cube
2 dashes Peychaud's bitters
dash Angostura bitters
dash Pernod
lemon peel

Fill two old-fashioned glasses with crushed ice to chill. Empty the ice from one glass and add the sugar cube, bitters and a dash of water. Crush the sugar and muddle until all the sugar is dissolved. Add the bourbon, several ice cubes and stir well. Empty the ice from the other glass. Splash a healthy dash of Pernod and swirl to coat the inside of the glass. Discard the excess and pour in the contents of the first glass. Twist the lemon peel over the glass, but don't place it in the drink.

A featured cocktail in the James Bond movie *Live and Let Die*, this labor-intensive cocktail was originally made with **Absinthe**. Absinthe has not been legally available in most countries since the early part of the 20th century.

(Even now it is only sold legally in Spain and the Czech Republic.) A strong bitter botanical liqueur, it was eventually determined that absinthe's hallucinatory effects were not caused by its alcohol content, but by a toxic substance present in its main ingredient, wormwood. Pernod and Anisette are good modern substitutes.

••

Silver Bullet Martini

Splash scotch
1½ oz. (45 mL) vodka
dash dry vermouth

Stir vodka and vermouth with ice and strain into a cocktail glass. Float scotch on top.

Ward Eight

2 oz. (60 mL) bourbon
1 oz. (30 mL) lemon juice
1 oz. (30 mL) orange juice
sugar syrup to taste
dash grenadine

Vigorously shake all the ingredients with ice, then strain into a chilled cocktail glass.

••

Similar to a Whisky Sour, this drink was apparently named for a voting district in Boston known for its hotly contested elections.

••

Whisky Sour

1 oz. (60 mL) blended whisky
2 oz. (30 mL) sour mix
maraschino cherry
orange slice

Combine whisky and sour mix in a shaker with cracked ice. Shake vigorously and strain into a sour glass, or serve with ice. Garnish with fruit.

This is probably one of the most popular mixed whisky drinks. You can make a sour mix yourself, as recommended on page 18, or you can avail yourself of one of those handy premixes.

Whisky and . . . As adaptable as whisky may be, many people enjoy it more simply. Straight scotch is a classic, though these days, people are a little more interested in type and brand. Single-malt scotch is a much-discussed topic.

Others enjoy their whisky with the addition of only one or two other elements – ice, soda, water being the usual suspects. For example, a **John Collins** is blended whisky or bourbon and club soda with the juice of half a lime and a splash of sugar syrup. Blended whisky, especially Canadian, and soda is popular, as is scotch and soda, and scotch and water. The whisky and soda drinks are usually tall, served with ice in a Collins glass, while scotch and soda or water drinks are usually served in the shorter old-fashioned glasses, with or without ice. Rye whisky and ginger ale or cola is also perennially acceptable.

 CANADIAN WHISKY SPECIALS

Suitable for patriotic occasions . . .

Canadian Cocktail

1½ oz. (45 mL) Canadian whisky
1/2 oz. (15 mL) Cointreau
1/2 tsp. (2.5 mL) superfine sugar
bitters

Combine all and shake well with ice. Strain into a cocktail glass.

Irish Canadian

1½ oz. (45 mL) Canadian whisky
1/2 oz. (15 mL) Irish Mist

Shake well with ice, then strain into a cocktail glass.

Saskatoon Stinger

2 oz. (60 mL) Canadian whisky
1 oz. (30 mL) peppermint schnapps
lemon twist

Stir whisky and schnapps with ice in an old-fashioned glass. Garnish with lemon.

Trois Rivières

1½ oz. (45 mL) Canadian whisky
3/4 oz. (22 mL) Dubonnet
1/2 oz. (15 mL) Triple Sec
orange peel

Shake all with ice and strain into an old-fashioned glass filled with ice. Twist orange peel over drink and add.

FYI

• *Most memorable whisky movie moment:*
  "Is your husband working on a case?"
      "Yeah, a case of Scotch."

> – *Myrna Loy to a reporter in* The Thin Man
> *(1934)*

• *Literary references to whisky:*
  "Freedom and whisky gang thegither!"

> – The Author's Earnest Cry and Prayer, *by Robert Burns, who became known as the "Whisky Poet"*

- *World's largest producer of distilled spirits:*
  Seagram's

- *World's largest malt whisky distillery:*
  Suntory of Japan

- *World's most expensive single-malt whisky:*
  Glenfiddich's 50-year-old

- *Most questionable name for a whisky drink:*
  Not a vast array to choose from. Perhaps whisky drinkers prefer to tell it like it is. One questionable selection is Roadkill, a shooter consisting of equal parts Irish whiskey, bourbon and Demerara rum.

- *Most used whisky-related phrase:*
  "It's the real McCoy." This phrase is used to describe anything that's genuine. Originally, it referred to scotch run into the United States, during Prohibition, by William McCoy. He had a reputation for delivering good, authentic Scotch.

All that they can be

Liquor has long enjoyed a relationship with the military, regardless of each other's fluctuating reputations. During the American Civil War, President Lincoln was forced to answer for General Grant's considerable consumption of whisky. Lincoln responded that, given Grant's considerable military success, perhaps all of his generals would be better off drinking Grant's favorite brand.

CHAPTER EIGHT

Brandy, cognac and Armagnac

At one time called *eau de vie*, or water of life, brandy was probably the first spirit produced after the invention of the still. Brandy has a long reputation as a tonic, its medicinal properties considered almost magical. The miniature brandy kegs carried by the St. Bernard rescue dog squads in the Alps are legend, even to viewers of Saturday morning cartoons.

BRANDY SAVVY: HISTORY, PRODUCTION AND STORAGE

The word brandy is derived from a Dutch term, **Brandewijn**, which means "burnt wine." One story of brandy's birth credits a Dutch shipmaster in the sixteenth century who was attempting to evade the heavy taxes imposed upon wine transported from France. He decided that if he removed the water by boiling it down and made a concentrate, he could reconstitute the liquor back in Holland. Likely, though, the practice had been started long before by farmers who boiled their surplus wine production down in order to save space. Written reference to it can be found at least as far back as 1250. Waste not, want not, in this case led to a new spirit that most people thought tasted better than the old wine.

Production Basically brandy is wine made even better through distillation and aging. Cognac and Armagnac are two types of grape brandy from France. Like champagne, their names reflect the regions they are from. Cognac and Armagnac set the standard for all other grape brandies. French brandy, in general, is held in high regard, though many wine-producing countries also make quite reputable grape brandy.

The general term *brandy* also refers to distillates based on fruits other than grape, for example, apricots, cherries, pears or raspberries. These fruit-based brandies are labelled as such.

Cognac Though all cognac is distilled in the same way and comes from a specific, legally defined region, not all cognac tastes the same. Partly this is to do with aging; partly this is because the region where cognac is produced straddles both northern and southern climate zones. Also, the soil in each part of the region is different, so that the wine they use to begin with is different in each area.

New, unaged wine is put into a pot still, the design of which has remained unchanged since the seventeenth century. Cognac results from two separate distillations.

The first distillation is called the *premier chauffe*. Both the first liquid to emerge and the final liquid to emerge are taken away. Only the centre part, known as the heart, or *brouillis*, will move on to the second distillation. Again, during the second distillation, the *bonne chauffe*, the first and final liquids will be separated out. Only the heart of the second distillation moves on to be aged. At this stage, new brandy is colorless and not particularly pleasant-tasting.

Slow and meticulous aging is required for the smooth, flavorful experience that brandy lovers relish. Casks made of aged oak from the Limousin natural forest are preferred. Casks made from oak from the Français forest are sometimes acceptable, but only for short-term storage. Storage is usually in storehouses that are slightly damp.

Best customer award goes to . . .

Since the casks are porous, a certain percentage of alcohol evaporates into thin air, millions of dollars worth annually. The distillers manage to remain philosophical about this, calling it *la part des anges* – "the angels' share." The distillers also maintain that the sun is their best customer.

After aging a minimum of 30 months, though possibly up to 50 years, nearly all cognacs have to be diluted with distilled water. Blending also usually occurs. Final touches include a little caramel for color and a little sugar syrup for softness. Cognac is also filtered for clarity before bottling. Unlike wine, but like other distilled spirits, no further aging takes place once brandy is bottled.

Armagnac Armagnac is another popular grape brandy from a specific area in France. It is produced in a still that is somewhat unique to the Armagnac region. In a modification of the continuous still, neutral white wine is distilled a single time. Aging takes place in cool, dark cellars in dark-colored casks made of Monlezum oak. A sappy oak from the forests of Bas-Armagnac, this wood imparts color.

Armagnac ages more quickly than cognac. After anywhere from one to 20 years blending will occur, then bottling, and no further aging will take place. Armagnac is appreciated for its strong, earthy fragrance and flavor.

LABEL TERMINOLOGY

The older the brandy, the more expensive it will be.

Armagnac

Three Stars: matured in cask from one to three years
VSOP: stands for very superior old pale, four years in cask
VO: stands for very old, indicates aging for five years; also labelled **Hors d'Age**

Cognac

Three Star or **VS:** (very special) means three to five years cask aging
VSOP: (very superior old pale) means cask maturation of seven to 17 years; also labelled **VO** or **Réserve**
XO: (extra old) also labelled **Grand Réserve Napolean**, **Hors d'Age**, **Royal**; cask matured 20 years or more

Storage Since brandies should be served at room temperature, store them in a cool, dry space. An opened bottle of brandy should last for two years.

BRANDY CLASSICS

Cognac and Armagnac have, over the years, both acquired places of honor as ceremonial after-dinner drinks. Slowly swirled in crystal snifters, warmed by hand, brandy is taken neat, reserved for special occasions.

Brandy can also be combined with mixers. Some enjoy it with soda water, ginger ale or lemonade. Other combinations create cocktails that can be enjoyed anytime. In France there is a custom of drinking Calvados, an apple brandy, in the middle of a meal in order to enhance appetite.

Apricot Brandy Sour

2 oz. (60 mL) apricot brandy
1 oz. (30 mL) lemon juice
1 tsp. (5 mL) sugar syrup (to taste)
lemon slice

Combine all the liquids and shake vigorously with crushed ice. Strain and pour into a chilled cocktail glass. Garnish with lemon.

Alexander's Sister

1½ oz. (45 mL) brandy
1 oz. (30 mL) white Crème de Menthe
1 oz. (30 mL) heavy cream

Combine ingredients and shake with cracked ice. Strain into chilled cocktail glass.

••

From the **Brandy Alexander** clan, another variation substitutes Kahlúa for the Crème de Menthe.

••

B & B

1 oz. (30 mL) cognac
1 oz. (30 mL) Bénédictine

Pour into a brandy snifter and swirl to blend.

••

Bénédictine is the oldest liqueur still produced. Containing more than 30 herbs and spices, Bénédictine's marriage with cognac is a fragrant classic not to be missed. The manufacturers of Bénédictine also make a ready-made B & B.

••

Brandy Alexander

1½ oz. (45 mL) brandy
1 oz. (30 mL) Crème de Cacao
1 oz. (30 mL) heavy cream

Shake all the ingredients with cracked ice and strain into a chilled cocktail glass. You may wish to top off with a nutmeg or cinnamon garnish

Chicago

1½ oz. (45 mL) brandy
dash Curaçao
dash Angostura bitters
champagne
lemon wedge
superfine sugar

Rim a chilled wine glass with lemon wedge and sugar. Combine brandy, Curaçao and bitters in a mixing glass with ice. Stir then strain into serving glass. Top up with champagne.

French 75

1½ oz. (45 mL) cognac
1/2 oz. (15 mL) sugar syrup (to taste)
champagne
juice of 1/2 lemon
lemon twist

Combine cognac, lemon juice and sugar syrup with cracked ice and shake. Strain into a chilled highball glass. Top up with cold champagne.

•••

This drink was originally made with gin and champagne; however, in the French trenches of World War I, gin was scarce while cognac was available. Soldiers found this combination quite enjoyable.

•••

Hawaiian Night

1 oz. (30 mL) light rum
1/4 oz. (8 mL) cherry-flavored brandy
pineapple juice

In a highball glass, half filled with ice, mix rum with pineapple juice. Float the brandy on top.

Jack Rose

2 oz. (60 mL) Applejack
1/2 z. (15 mL) lime or lemon juice
1 tsp. (5 mL) grenadine

Shake all ingredients with cracked ice and strain into a chilled cocktail glass.

Applejack is a very pale apple brandy produced in the United States. **Calvados**, from France, is probably the most popular apple brandy internationally, and would certainly be a suitable substitute.

Mayfair Cocktail

1 oz. (30 mL) cognac
1 oz. (30 mL) Dubonnet rouge
1/2 oz. (15 mL) lime juice
1 tsp. (5 mL) sugar syrup
a few dashes of Angostura bitters
orange peel

Shake all, except the orange peel, with cracked ice and strain into a chilled cocktail glass. Twist the orange peel over the drink and drop it in.

Peach Irish

1½ oz. (45 mL) Irish whiskey
1/2 cup (125 mL) fresh lime juice
1 oz. (30 mL) apricot brandy
1 tbsp. (15 mL) superfine sugar
1 ripe peach, peeled, pitted, sliced
dash vanilla extract

Combine all in a blender with crushed ice. A grown-up Smoothie.

Sidecar

1½ oz. (45 mL) brandy
3/4 oz. (22 mL) Curaçao
1/2 oz. (15 mL) lemon juice

Vigorously shake the ingredients with ice. Strain and pour into a chilled cocktail glass.

A Sidecar can be made with other liquors but the original, with brandy, is a classic.

FEATURED DRINKS:
SHOOTERS AND POUSSE-CAFÉS

There are innumerable ways to enjoy the variety of brandies available. Brandy is found in old favorites like such as **Singapore Sling** and **Zombie**, classics as listed here, and it is a favorite component in some of the trendier shooters and pousse-cafés.

Shooters are small mixed concoctions meant to be downed in one gulp. **Pousse-Cafés** are more complicated. Popular back in the 1840s, they have enjoyed several waves of popularity ever since. They are tricky to make because the point of the drink is to layer the liquors so that they appear to be floating on top of each other. This can be accomplished by pouring the liquids over the back of a spoon in order to break their fall into the glass. Practice makes perfect . . .

After 8 *(shooter)*

1/2 oz. (15 mL) coffee brandy
1/2 oz. (15 mL) Irish Cream
1/2 oz. (15 mL) Crème de Menthe (white or green)

Shake all ingredients with ice and strain into a shot glass.

Cherry Bomb *(shooter)*

1/2 oz. (15 mL) cherry brandy
1/2 oz. (15 mL) rum
1/2 oz. (15 mL) sour mix

Shake everything with ice. Strain and pour into a shot glass.

Good and Plenty *(shooter)*

1 oz. (30 mL) blackberry brandy
1 oz. (30 mL) Anisette

Shake with ice. Strain and pour into a shot glass.

Pousse-Café à la Française

1/4 oz. (8 mL) green Chartreuse
1/4 oz. (8 mL) maraschino liqueur
1/4 oz. (8 mL) cherry brandy
1/4 oz. (8 mL) Kummel

Pour each of these ingredients slowly to layer, in the order given. Use a pony or pousse-café glass.

Yellow Morning *(pousse-café)*

1/3 oz. (10 mL) Crème de Banane
1/3 oz. (10 mL) Cherry Heering
1/3 oz. (10 mL) cognac

Layer these ingredients in the order given, Crème de Banane first, Cognac last.

FYI

- *Most memorable brandy movie moment:*
  In *The Big Sleep* (1946), an old general reminisces about how he used to like his brandy: "I used to like mine with champagne – champagne cold as Valley Forge, and with three ponies of brandy under it." Sounds like memories of a French 75.

  Somewhat less savory was the central role assumed by a Brandy Alexander in luring an unsuspecting teetotaller in *Days of Wine and Roses* (1962).

  In *Titanic* (1997), recipient of several Academy Awards, including best picture, the last drink ordered is a brandy.

- *Literary references to brandy:*
  " . . . he who aspires to be a hero must drink brandy."

  – Samuel Johnson

- Oldest cognac house in France:

  – Martell

CHAPTER NINE

Liqueurs

Colorful, flavorful and sweet, liqueurs have been with us for a very long time. In fact, the production methods and materials of some very popular liqueurs have remained unchanged for hundreds of years. One liqueur, Chartreuse, is still made by the same order of monks, the Carthusian Brothers, who first made it in 1605. Bénédictine, although it has not been made by monks since the end of the eighteenth century, is still made according to the original recipe from 1510.

LIQUEUR SAVVY: HISTORY, PRODUCTION AND STORAGE

Liqueurs were first designed as medicines or general tonics. The use of roots, seeds, herbs, spices, fruits and flowers has always been associated with therapy of one sort or another. Various types of liqueurs were known as far back as ancient Greece and Rome. Today's habit of serving liqueurs after dinner is a throwback to the days when liqueurs were prescribed as digestive aids.

Although liqueurs have been around for hundreds of years, they really came into their own in the Middle Ages. The discovery of distilling techniques made for a practical method of preserving extracts of fruits and herbs. Many people made their own liqueurs at home by adding sugar and fruit to brandy or any other alcohol at hand. It is still possible to do so, but generally it is the guarded secret-recipe formulas that taste best.

All liqueurs contain a base spirit. This could be a neutral alcohol, brandy, rum, whisky, rice spirit or other alcohol. There will also be raw materials for flavoring. These elements could be herbs, barks, roots, flowers, seeds, fruit and even dairy products. All liqueurs are sweetened by beet sugar, sugar syrup or honey, and must by law contain at least 2.5 percent sugar by weight, though most contain much more. Also, for a variety of reasons, psychological and marketing included, most liqueurs are colored, usually with natural vegetable matter.

To produce a liqueur, natural substances are combined with alcohol in one of four ways (some liqueurs use more than one method):

1. Infusion The natural substances are steeped in water, then combined with alcohol.

2. Maceration Mostly associated with fruit liqueurs, the flavoring agents are steeped in an alcohol, such as brandy. This steeping process will take longer than the infusion method.

3. Distillation This method is usually used with botanical flavoring agents, plants, seeds, herbs and roots. The flavoring materials are steeped with alcohol, usually for a couple of days, then the mixture is distilled in a modified pot still.

4. Percolation Just like perked coffee, alcohol is pumped up and dripped through the flavoring agents, plants, leaves and herbs. This pumping and percolation process will be repeated for weeks until all the flavorings have been extracted.

While these methods have remained virtually unchanged for centuries, the liqueur industry has, somewhat ironically, been a source of more recent technological breakthroughs. For example, dairy-cream liqueurs, such as Irish Cream, were the result of an innovation that made it possible to homogenize dairy cream with alcohol for an end product that has little or no need for refrigeration.

Liqueurs can be divided into two very broad categories: generic and proprietary. The proprietary types are specialty liqueurs made from top-secret formulas, many of them handed down through countless generations. Some examples include Bénédictine, Chartreuse, Cointreau, Drambuie, Frangelico, Grand Marnier and Kahlúa. Generic liqueurs are the most basic flavors that can be made by any distiller. This doesn't mean that they are inferior, just that the recipe is no secret. Amaretto, Anisette, Crème de Menthe, Curaçao, Sambuca and Triple Sec are examples of popular generic liqueurs.

 ## Silence is golden . . . or green

The distillers of Chartreuse, a sweet, very fragrant green or golden yellow liqueur, are a silent order of Carthusian monks. Although known to be a blend of around 130 herbs, the liqueur's formula is so secret that even the civilian CEO is not allowed in the distillation rooms. Actually no one, aside from the chief distiller and his two aides, is allowed into those rooms. Apparently, in an effort to thwart would-be spies, the brothers purposely order unnecessary herbs, or huge surpluses of herbs, in order to obscure which ingredients are really essential. The monks themselves are only permitted to drink Chartreuse three times a year.

For storage a cool, dry place is preferable. A feature of liqueurs is that they have a relatively long shelf-life even after they have been opened. An opened bottle of liqueur should be fine for three years or more.

TYPES OF LIQUEURS

The number of liqueurs available today is astounding. Here is a short list describing some of the most popular. In the United States you will find that liqueurs are called *cordials*.

Advocaat is originally from the Netherlands, made from grape brandy, egg yolks and sugar. Thick and creamy, it also comes in flavored varieties.

Alizé is a cognac base blended with passion fruit.

Amaretto dates back to 1525 in Saronna, Italy. It is an almond and apricot-flavored liqueur.

Anisette gets its licorice flavor from aniseed. It has a pure spirit base.

Bénédictine is a double-distilled cognac brandy, mixed with more than 30 herbs and plants. Though no longer produced by monks, each bottle acknowledges it religious connections with the initials DOM for Deo Optimo Maximo, which means "God, most good, most great."

Chambord combines raspberries, herbs and additional fruit with honey.

Chartreuse is highly flavored and fragrant due to the mix of about 130 herbs and spices and a brandy base. Green Chartreuse is colored with chlorophyll, and has a higher alcohol content than yellow. Yellow Chartreuse is colored with saffron, and is sweeter than the green.

Cointreau is a clear liqueur made from natural spirits plus Mediterranean and West Indian oranges. It was developed by two candy makers in France, Edouard and Aldolphe Cointreau, who originally called their liqueur Triple Sec, but it was imitated so freely that the brothers established the House of Cointreau in 1849.

Crèmes

Although *crème* literally means "cream," when applied to liqueurs it means that the drink will taste distinctly of one flavor, the one designated in its name. For example, crème de menthe tastes like mint. As well as being frequent cocktail ingredients, the crèmes are delicious served *frappé*, with crushed ice.

Liqueur	Flavor
Crème d'Ananas	pineapple
Crème de Banane	banana
Crème de Cacao	chocolate
Crème de Café	coffee
Crème de Cassis	black currants
Crème de Ciel	orange
Crème de Fraise	strawberry
Crème de Framboise	raspberry
Crème de Noisette	hazelnut
Crème de Noyaux	almond
Crème de Poire	pear
Crème Yvette	violet

Curaçao is a bitter orange-flavored liqueur. It was originally devised by British naval doctors hoping to prevent scurvy. Unfortunately orange peel distilled in alcohol is not a good way to preserve vitamin C, but the liqueur was popular anyway. It is produced in a variety of colors: blue, green, orange, clear, even brown.

Drambuie is one of those secret-formula recipes that include malt whiskies, heather honey, herbs and spices. The original recipe is credited to Bonnie Prince Charlie. It seems that the Prince gave the recipe as a gift for loyalty to Captain John MacKinnon in 1746 or so, and it is made by the MacKinnon family still.

Frangelico tastes predominantly of hazelnuts, though it contains an infusion of berries, herbs and flowers.

Galliano is a blend made from more than 30 herbs, flowers, berries, roots, vanilla and anise. First prepared in 1896, Galliano was not popularized until the 1970s when it was marketed as a key ingredient in the Harvey Wallbanger.

Goldschlager is a cinnamon schnapps liqueur with real flakes of 24-karat gold floating about inside.

Grand Marnier is an elegant orange-flavored liqueur. The flavoring agents are macerated in cognac, distilled and then blended with aged cognac and sugar syrup. The Lapostolle family launched the Grand Marnier company in 1827.

Irish Cream is a relative newcomer to the liqueur scene, launched in 1974. The taste is of fresh cream, Irish whiskey, vanilla and cocoa. Bailey's is the best known but there are other brands.

Kahlúa is a blend of cane spirit, coffee and vanilla. Originally from Mexico, it is one of the best-selling liqueurs worldwide.

Kummel is flavored with caraway seeds, cumin, orris root and fennel.

Midori is another newcomer. It was created in 1978 by Suntory of Japan. Made with musk melon, it is quite sweet and very green.

Ouzo is an aniseed-flavored liqueur from Greece. It is not as sweet as Anisette.

Pernod is a licorice-flavored liqueur. It is similar to absinthe, but without the controversial wormwood component.

Sambuca tastes predominantly of licorice, though it is also flavored with elderberry. In Italy it is traditional to serve Sambuca with three coffee beans floating in it. The beans are then flamed in the liqueur and this lends the liqueur additional flavor.

Sloe Gin is flavored with sloeberries, a small, wild plum-like fruit that grows in France.

Southern Comfort was devised in the United States, originally with a bourbon-whisky base, along with peaches, oranges and several other ingredients added. It is enjoyed worldwide and is now made, under license, in a few different countries.

Tia Maria is a coffee-flavored liqueur with a Jamaican rum base. This liqueur is traditionally served with cream floating on top.

Triple Sec is an orange-flavored liqueur.

LIQUEUR DRINK CLASSICS

Most liqueurs can be drunk simply: neat, and on their own. Some liqueurs, especially the creams and crèmes, taste best chilled or on ice.

But many, if not all liqueurs, are also great team players. They are key ingredients in many cocktails. Several liqueur cocktail recipes are found throughout this book listed by the alcohol with which the liqueur is mixed. Don't forget previously mentioned classics such as B & B (page 86), Black Russian (page 58), Brandy Alexander (page 86), Hummer (page 48), Long Island Iced Tea (page 35), Mai Tai (page 50), Rusty Nail (page 77) and Singapore Sling (page 42).

Alabama Slammer

1 oz. (30 mL) Amaretto
1 oz. (30 mL) Southern Comfort
1/2 oz. (15 mL) Sloe gin
dash lemon juice

Stir Amaretto, Southern Comfort and Sloe gin with ice in a highball glass. Add the lemon juice and stir well.

•••

This concoction can also be strained into a shot glass and served as a shooter.
•••

B52

1/2 oz. (15 mL) Kahlúa
1/2 oz. (15 mL) Irish Cream
1/2 oz. (15 mL) Grand Marnier

Shake with ice, and strain into a rocks glass over ice. This can also be served as a shooter or, for those with a steady hand, it could be served layered as a pousse-café. Layer the liqueurs in the order given.

Friar Tuck

2 oz. (60 mL) Frangelico
2 oz. (60 mL) lemon juice
1 tsp. (5 mL) grenadine
orange slice
maraschino cherry

Shake the liquids with cracked ice. Pour into a chilled rocks glass and garnish with fruit.

Grasshopper

1 oz. (30 mL) green Crème de Menthe
1 oz. (30 mL) white Crème de Menthe
1 oz. (30 mL) light cream

Shake vigorously with ice, or combine in a blender with ice. Strain into a chilled cocktail glass.

Kamikaze

1 oz. (30 mL) Triple Sec
1 oz. (30 mL) vodka
1 oz. (30 mL) lime juice

Combine everything with cracked ice. Shake and strain into a chilled cocktail glass.

Margarita

1 oz. (30 mL) tequila
1 oz. (30 mL) Cointreau
1 oz. (30 mL) sour mix
2–3 dashes of lime juice
lime wheel

Pour all liquids into a mixing glass filled with crushed ice. Shake vigorously and strain into a chilled cocktail glass. Some prefer it on the rocks. Garnish with lime. Some drinkers like this served in a salt-rimmed glass, or a glass rimmed with a half-salt, half-sugar combination.

Margaritas are usually considered tequila drinks, yet they were created by a woman who apparently loved Cointreau as much as tequila. There are variations, though, both regarding its origins and the proportions. The manufacturers of Cointreau designated 1998 as the official fiftieth anniversary of the invention of the Margarita.

Pink Squirrel

    1 oz. (30 mL) Crème de Noyaux
    1 oz. (30 mL) white Crème de Cacao
    1 oz. (30 mL) cream

Shake all with ice and strain into a chilled cocktail glass.

Shady Lady

    1 oz. (30 mL) melon liqueur
    1 oz. (30 mL) vodka or tequila
    3 oz. (90 mL) grapefruit juice
    thin slice of lime

Combine the liquids in a shaker with ice. Shake and serve over ice in a highball glass. Garnish with lime.

Sloe Gin Fizz

    2 oz. (60 mL) Sloe gin
    1/2 oz. (15 mL) lemon juice
    1 tsp. (5 mL) sugar syrup
    club soda
    lemon slice

Mix Sloe gin, lemon juice and sugar syrup with cracked ice. Pour into a chilled Collins glass. Top up with soda and garnish with lemon.

White Lady

 1½ oz. (45 mL) gin
 3/4 oz. (22 mL) Cointreau
 3/4 oz. (22 mL) lemon juice

Shake everything with cracked ice and strain into a chilled cocktail glass.

•••

Prior to 1929, a White Lady paired white Crème de Menthe with Cointreau. For some reason Harry, of Harry's New York Bar in Paris, started using gin, and this combination became the favorite.

•••

LIQUEUR SHOOTERS

Liqueur shooters are particularly popular with the young bar crowd. Although potent, they still taste a bit like candy.

Beam Me Up Scotty

 1/2 oz. (15 mL) Kahlúa
 1/2 oz. (15 mL) Irish Cream
 1/2 oz. (15 mL) Crème de Banane

Shake with ice and strain into a shot glass.

Dublin Double

 3/4 oz. (22 mL) Amaretto
 3/4 oz. (22 mL) Irish Cream

Mix, then pour into a shot glass. This is also enjoyable on the rocks.

Candy Apple

 1/2 oz. (15 mL) apple schnapps
 1/2 oz. (15 mL) cinnamon schnapps
 1/2 oz. (15 mL) apple juice

Shake with ice and strain into a shot glass.

Girl Scout Cookie

1½ oz. (45 mL) peppermint schnapps
1½ oz. (45 mL) coffee liqueur
3 oz. (90 mL) 10% cream

Shake with ice and strain into two shot glasses.

Jelly Bean

3/4 oz. (22 mL) Anisette
3/4 oz. (22 mL) blackberry-flavored brandy

Mix with ice and strain into a shot glass.

M & M

3/4 oz. (22 mL) Kahlúa
3/4 oz. (22 mL) Amaretto

In a shot glass, layer the Amaretto over the Kahlúa.

Peppermint Patty

1/2 oz. (15 mL) peppermint schnapps
1/2 oz. (15 mL) Crème de Cacao
1 oz. (30 mL) cream

Stir with ice and strain into a shot glass. This is also enjoyable on the rocks.

- *Oldest existing liqueur still produced:*
  Bénédictine

- *Only brand of liqueur to be named by a bartender:*
  Southern Comfort.
      A bartender in Missouri re-marketed an older drink, known as Cuffs and Buttons, and renamed it Southern Comfort. The blend of peaches and bourbon was even more popular than straight bourbon.

- *First liqueur ever formulated:*
  Hippocras

- *World's best-selling liqueur:*
  Bailey's Irish Cream

- *Naughty name award:*
  Orgasm and **Sex on the Beach** are two, though there are others that might make many people blush.

Orgasm

1/2 oz. (15 mL) Irish cream
1/2 oz. (15 mL) Amaretto
1/2 oz. (15 mL) coffee liqueur

Shake with ice and strain into a shot glass.

Sex on the Beach

1 oz. (30 mL) vodka
1/2 oz. (15 mL) Midori
1/2 oz. (15 mL) Chambord
1½ oz. (45 mL) pineapple juice
1½ oz. (45 mL) cranberry juice

Shake all with ice and pour into a highball glass. This combination also has been reincarnated as a shooter. Reduce the juices to 1 oz. (30 mL) each, and this is enough for two shots.

CHAPTER TEN

Concoctions

The multi-ingredient drink has always represented something more than a mere beverage. Those who just want a drink of liquor take it straight, with water or soda. To build a cocktail or punch, however, implies a desire to invoke an image, create an atmosphere or embrace a tradition.

TROPICAL DELIGHTS

Tropical drinks are a perennial favorite. They help create the exotic atmosphere of a relaxing vacation, in some earthly paradise. At one time, especially after World War II and until the 1970s, tropical motif theme bars were particularly popular. In one of the most popular television shows of its day, *I Love Lucy*, Lucy's husband, Ricky, was the headline performer at the Tropicana. There aren't too many Coconut Groves or Kon-Tiki Rooms left anymore, but the drinks they served and inspired are still popular.

Several tropical drink recipes have already been given. Look for a **Singapore Sling** recipe on page 42. Don't forget the **Daiquiri** (page 48), **Mai Tai** (page 50), **Piña Colada** (page 51) and **Zombie** (page 52) recipes.

Many tropical drinks are big, tall thirst quenchers, so they are good choices for summer entertaining. Tropical drinks are high in alcohol content, however, so beware.

Bahama Mama

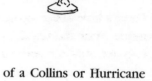

1½ oz. (45 mL) light rum
1½ oz. (45 mL) gold rum
1½ oz. (45 mL) dark rum
2 oz. (60 mL) sour mix
2 oz. (60 mL) pineapple juice
2½ oz. (75 mL) orange juice
dash grenadine
maraschino cherry
orange slice

Pour a dash of grenadine in the bottom of a Collins or Hurricane glass. Shake all the other liquids in a mixing glass with ice and pour into the prepared Collins or Hurricane glass. Garnish with fruit.

Blue Hawaiian

1 oz. (30 mL) light rum
1 oz. (30 mL) blue Curaçao
1 oz. (30 mL) cream of coconut
2 oz. (60 mL) pineapple juice
maraschino cherry
orange slice

Process liquids in a blender with about 1/2 cup (125 mL) of crushed ice. Blend on low speed for approximately 15 seconds. Pour into a stemmed glass and garnish with fruit.

Chi Chi

2 oz. (60 mL) vodka
1½ oz. (45 mL) cream of coconut
5 oz. (150 mL) pineapple juice
maraschino cherry
pineapple slice

Blend liquids with about 1 cup (250 mL) of crushed ice on medium to high speed in a blender. Pour into a stemmed goblet and garnish with fruit.

Coco-Loco

1 oz. (30 mL) tequila
1 oz. (30 mL) rum
1 oz. (30 mL) gin
1/2 oz. (15 mL) grenadine
a whole coconut
twist lemon or lime

Carve a hole in the top of the coconut. Be sure not to spill the juice inside. Pour the tequila, rum, gin and grenadine directly into the coconut. Add ice and stir. Drop in a twist of lemon or lime and serve with a long straw.

Gorilla Punch

1 oz. (30 mL) vodka
1/2 oz. (15 mL) blue Curaçao
2 oz. (60 mL) orange juice
2 oz. (60 mL) pineapple juice
maraschino cherry

Shake all the liquid ingredients with ice and strain into an old-fashioned glass filled with ice. Garnish with cherry.

Honolulu Cocktail

1½ oz. (45 mL) gin
1 tsp. (5 mL) orange juice
1 oz. (30 mL) pineapple juice
1 tsp. (5 mL) lime juice
1 tsp. (5 mL) lemon juice
1/2 tsp. (2.5 mL) superfine sugar

Shake everything with ice and pour into a chilled cocktail glass.

Hurricane

1 oz. (30 mL) light rum
1 oz. (30 mL) gold rum
1/2 oz. (15 mL) passion fruit syrup
1/2 oz. (15 mL) lime juice

Shake everything with ice and strain into a chilled cocktail glass.

Reggae

2 oz. (60 mL) vodka
1/2 oz. (15 mL) Crème de Banane
1 oz. (30 mL) orange juice
1/2 oz. (15 mL) grapefruit juice
1/2 oz. (15 mL) pineapple juice
1/2 tsp. (2.5 mL) grenadine
dash orange bitters
maraschino cherry
orange slice
pineapple wedge

Reserve the fruit for garnish. Vigorously shake all liquids with ice. Strain into a highball glass filled with fresh ice. Garnish with fruit.

Scorpion

2 oz. (60 mL) light rum
1 oz. (30 mL) brandy
2 oz. (60 mL) orange juice
1/2 oz. (15 mL) lemon juice
1/2 oz. (15 mL) Crème de Noyaux
maraschino cherry
orange slice

Combine everything but the orange slice and cherry in a blender with about 1 cup (250 mL) of ice. Blend until smooth. Pour into an old-fashioned glass and garnish with fruit.

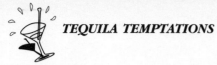

TEQUILA TEMPTATIONS

Tequila drinks are really a subset of tropical drinks, but they deserve separate mention for a few reasons. Tequila has something of an outlaw reputation as a liquor. It is falsely, yet commonly, linked to undesirable qualities (worms in the bottle and hallucinogenic properties), though this seems to lure the younger bar crowd. While the '80s and '90s saw liquor sales in general go down, tequila sales have actually gone up. This is particularly true in the United States. Even Canadians enjoy Margaritas and Tequila Sunrises, and it is hard to imagine a trend in the United States that doesn't result in an echo north of the border.

Tequila Basics   Tequila is made from one very specific type of the agave plant. It is a succulent, and although there are more than 400 varieties, only *Agave tequiliana Weber*, known as blue agave, may be used for tequila production.

In ancient times, the Aztecs considered the agave plant to be sacred. They used its fibers to make rope, cloth and a rough paper. The leaves were thatched into roofs, thorns were used as needles, and sap was fermented into a beverage. Distillation was introduced by the Spanish.

Tequila is so named because most of it comes from around the town of Tequila. The Mexican government strictly demarcates the five-state region where tequila can be produced.

Production   The agave plants take between eight and 12 years to mature. Optimum growing conditions include an arid environment and silicate-based soil.

It is the inner core of the plant, which can weigh between 100 and 150 pounds, that is harvested. The core, called a piña, is quartered and placed in huge brick ovens for about a day and a half of baking, then a day and a half of cooling. The baked piñas are crushed and the liquid is fermented in wood vats. Distillation can be in pot stills or continuous column stills. If a tequila bottle does not state specifically *100% de Agave* or *100% blue agave*, then other sugars, usually sugarcane, may comprise up to 40 percent of the total sugar content before distillation.

Tequila doesn't require a lot of aging, but there are four styles that apply to both 100% de Agave and the mixed types. *Blanco*, also known as silver or white tequila, is clear and has either been bottled immediately, or minimally aged for no more than a couple of months in metal holding tanks. *Gold* has not been aged either, but it has had caramel added for color and smoothness. *Reposado* tequila has been wood-aged for between two and 12 months. Finally, *Añejo* style has been oak barrel-aged for at least a year. The cost of tequila increases with the amount of time it has been aged.

 ## So where's the worm?

There is *never* a worm included in a bottle of tequila. Worms are placed in bottles of mezcal. Mezcal is another liquor from Mexico, also made from agave, but not blue agave. Two types of worm are involved, both native to the agave plant. They are hand-harvested and added to mezcal as it is bottled. Over time, drink stories got mixed and many people, even tequila drinkers, mistakenly think they'll find a worm in a bottle of tequila.

Tequila drinks A couple of tequila-drink recipes can be found elsewhere in this book. Look in chapter 4 for Long Island Iced Tea (page 35) and in chapter 9 for a classic Margarita (page 98) and Shady Lady (page 99). The Coco-Loco (page 105) experience is described in this chapter, under tropical drinks.

Berta's Special

2 oz. (60 mL) tequila
1 tsp. (5 mL) sugar syrup or honey
1 egg white
juice of a lime
several dashes orange bitters
club soda
orange slice

Combine, and shake with ice, the tequila, sugar, egg white and lime juice. Pour into a Collins glass and top up with club soda. Garnish with lime.

••

This drink is also known as a **Taxco Fizz**.

••

Freddy Fudpucker

2 oz. (60 mL) tequila
4 oz. (120 mL) orange juice
1/2 oz. (15 mL) Galliano

Stir together tequila and orange juice in a Collins glass filled with ice. Pour the Galliano slowly over the back of a barspoon or teaspoon in order to float it on top of the drink. A tequila Wallbanger.

Frozen Margarita

1½ oz. (45 mL) white tequila
1/2 oz. (15 mL) Cointreau
1 oz. (30 mL) lime juice
2 cups (500 mL) crushed ice
coarse salt
lime wedge

Run the lime wedge around the rim of a large, chilled cocktail glass or wine goblet. Dip the rim in coarse salt (some prefer to use a half salt-half sugar mix). Place tequila, Cointreau, lime juice and ice in a blender. Blend until slushy, but not watery, then pour into the rimmed glass.

Monja Loco

1½ oz. (45 mL) white or gold tequila
1½ oz. (45 mL) Anisette

In an old-fashioned glass filled with ice, stir the ingredients to combine.

••

This is also known as a **Crazy Nun**.

••

Piña

 1½ oz. (45 mL) tequila
 3 oz. (90 mL) pineapple juice
 1 oz. (30 mL) lime juice
 1 tsp. (5 mL) sugar syrup or honey
 lime slice

Shake all liquids with cracked ice. Pour into a chilled old-fashioned glass and garnish with lime.

Spanish Moss

 1½ oz. (45 mL) tequila
 1 oz. (30 mL) coffee liqueur
 3 drops green Crème de Menthe

Shake tequila and coffee liqueur with ice and strain into a chilled cocktail glass. Float the three drops of crème de menthe on top.

Tequila Mockingbird

 1½ oz. (45 mL) white tequila
 1 tsp. (10 mL) white Crème de Menthe
 1 oz. (30 mL) lime juice

Shake with 3 or 4 ice cubes, then strain into a chilled cocktail glass.

Tequila Sunrise

 1½ oz. (45 mL) white or gold tequila
 1/2 oz. (15 mL) lime juice
 4 oz. (120 mL) orange juice
 3/4 oz. (22 mL) grenadine
 lime slice

Stir the first 3 ingredients together with ice in a Collins glass. Slowly pour the grenadine into the center of the drink and do not stir. Garnish with lime.

Tequila Shooters

Tequila has been customarily consumed as a shooter for a very long time, since before shooters were considered fashionable.

 **FEATURED DRINK**

The original authentic tequila shooter, a.k.a. Mexican Itch, a.k.a. Tequila Cruda

1½ oz. (45 mL) white tequila
lime wedge
pinch coarse salt

Pour tequila into a shot glass. Rub the lime wedge on the back of your left hand where your thumb and index finger meet. Sprinkle salt over the moistened area. Hold the lime wedge between the thumb and index finger of your left hand. Lick the salt off your hand. Swallow the tequila in one gulp and suck the lime wedge. Breathing will resume shortly.

This is often followed by a tequila chaser called Sangrita. If a Mexican food shop or section is in your vicinity, you could buy this pre-made.

Sangrita *(this yields several servings)*

2 cups (500 mL) tomato juice
1 cup (250 mL) orange juice
2 oz. (60 mL) lime juice
1 tsp. (10 mL) Tabasco sauce
1 tsp. (10 mL) minced onion
1 tsp. (10 mL) Worcestershire sauce
2–3 pinches of white pepper
pinch of celery salt

Combine everything in a blender. After thorough blending, strain into a container for chilling in the refrigerator. Serve in jigger or shot-sized portions.

Blue Shark

1/2 oz. (15 mL) tequila
1/2 oz. (15 mL) vodka
1/2 oz. (15 mL) blue Curaçao

Shake with ice and strain into a shot glass.

Cucaracha

1 oz. (30 mL) Kahlúa
1 oz. (30 mL) tequila

Layer in a shot glass.

Lizard Slime

1½ oz. (45 mL) tequila
1 tsp. (5 mL) Midori

Float the Midori on top of the tequila.

Mexican Flag

1/2 oz. (15 mL) Sloe gin
1/2 oz. (15 mL) white tequila
1/2 oz. (15 mL) green Crème de Menthe

Slowly pour each ingredient to layer them in the order given.

Prairie Fire

1½ oz. (45 mL) tequila
2–3 drops of Tabasco sauce

Combine in a shot glass.

Wet Spot

1 oz. (30 mL) tequila
1 oz. (30 mL) Irish Cream

Shake with ice and strain into a shot glass.

PUNCHES

Traditionally, punches were meant to showcase the ultimate care and hospitality a host could bestow upon guests. "Proud as punch" is a saying from an era when the punch bowl was a matter of pride. Although somewhat less appreciated in our day, a well-made and thoughtfully presented punch can still be festive.

There are two theories to explain the origins of the word *punch*. One claims that it is a shortening of word *puncheon*, a cask that holds about 70-80 gallons (280+ L). While punches are meant to serve several people, they aren't usually *this* big. The other theory claims that punch was derived from the Hindustani word *pãnch*, which means five. There is a certain rule-of-five which holds that a punch must have at least five ingredients: something sour, something sweet, something strong, something weak and spices. Apparently British ex-patriots living in India during the 1600s made a beverage that conformed to the rule-of-five. It consisted of lemon juice, sugar, fermented sap, water and tea.

The rule-of-five doesn't always apply anymore, but there are some handy tips that will make the most of your efforts; and there will be some occasions where you might want to serve a punch.

Punch Pointers

- Punch servings are about 4 oz. (120 mL). Caterers assume that the average person will have three punch servings at a party.
- Successful punches require premium ingredients. They were never meant to be a dumping ground for inferior products.
- Sugar does not mix easily into alcohol. (That is why so many drink recipes call for sugar syrup.) Dissolve any quantities of sugar that might be required into the juices or other mixers before you add the alcohol.
- While it may be possible to construct some punches ahead of time, don't add the liquor until 30-60 minutes before the party. The alcohol will start to evaporate.
- Champagne, sparkling wine and carbonated mixers should not be added until the last moment.

- Do not use ice cubes. They melt too fast and dilute the punch.
- Use blocks of ice or make an ice ring mold, or any other shape mold. The molds can be made more festive by freezing fruit or even flowers in the ice.

Ambrosia Punch *(serves about 8)*

20-oz. (600 mL) can crushed pineapple
15 oz. (450 mL) cream of coconut
2 cups (500 mL) apricot nectar
2 cups (500 mL) orange juice
1½ cups (375 mL) rum
4 cups (I L) club soda

Before combining, chill the juices and soda. Mix together the cream of coconut and the strained can of crushed pineapple in a blender. In the punch bowl, stir together the pureed mixture, nectar, juice, rum. Add soda just before serving. Serve over ice.

Bombay Punch *(serves about 20)*

1 cup (250 mL) lemon juice
1/2 cup (125 mL) lime juice
1 cup (250 mL) superfine sugar
4 cups (1 L) cognac
4 cups (1 L) sherry
1/2 cup (125 mL) Cointreau
1/2 cup (125 mL) maraschino liqueur
1/4 cup (65 mL) cherry brandy
4 bottles (750 mL each) chilled sparkling wine
8 cups (2 L) club soda
orange slices
maraschino cherries

Dissolve the sugar in the lemon and lime juices in a large punch bowl. Stir in the cognac, sherry, Cointreau, maraschino liqueur and the cherry brandy. Pour in the wine and club soda and serve immediately. Garnish with fruit.

Fishhouse Punch *(serves about 10)*

2 cups (500 mL) lemon juice
1 cup (250 mL) superfine sugar
1½ cups (375 mL) peach brandy
8 cups (2 L) rum
4 cups (1 L) brandy
4 cups (1 L) club soda

Stir well to dissolve the sugar in the lemon juice. Add the liquors and stir. Pour in the club soda at the last moment and add a large block of ice.

Planter's Punch *(serves about 10)*

4 cups (1 L) light rum
2 cups (500 mL) dark rum
2 cups (500 mL) fresh lime juice
2 cups (500 mL) sugar syrup
4 cups (1 L) club soda
orange slices
cherries

Except for the soda and fruit, stir the ingredients together in a punch bowl. Add an ice block and, just before serving, pour in the soda. Float the fruit for garnish.

Tropical Punch *(serves about 20)*

5 bottles white wine
1 lb. (400 g) brown sugar
4 cups (1 L) orange juice
2 cups (500 mL) lemon juice
5 sliced bananas
1 pineapple, chopped
4 cups (1 L) light rum
2 cups (500 mL) dark rum
2 cups (500 mL) Crème de Banane
assorted sliced fruit

Combine wine, sugar, juices, sliced bananas and pineapple in a very large bowl. Cover and let sit overnight. An hour before serving, add rums and liqueurs. Strain into a large punch bowl. Float a block or two of ice and garnish with fruit.

GRANDE FINALE: POUSSE-CAFÉS

No matter what the occasion, a spectacular way to cap off the event is to serve pousse-cafés.

Literally, *pousse-café* translated from French means "push down the coffee," and the two go together quite nicely. These little layered specialty drinks are not new. We know that they were popular in the American south in the mid-1800s. The first recipe listed in a 1927 Canadian guide to mixing drinks is not merely a pousse-café, but it is a pousse-café that is to be ignited before serving. (As if layering liqueurs is not challenging enough!)

The success of a pousse-café depends on a few factors: practice and a steady hand. Taste is another consideration – the layers need to taste good together. Appearance is also an important element. They need to look good. Finally, it boils down to specific gravity. Different liqueurs, liquors and other ingredients have different specific gravities. Basically, the "heavier" liquids must be layered under the "lighter" liquids.

If you want to experiment with building your own pousse-cafés, the various liqueur manufacturers could probably supply you with their own specific gravity list. There is also information available on the Internet.

Here is a generic list, from heaviest to lightest. To successfully float one on top of another, the ingredients should be separated by three. For example, it is highly likely that Crème de Noyaux will not float on top of Anisette, but Crème de Banane will.

1.	Crème de Cacao	14.	Drambuie
2.	Anisette	15.	Bénédictine
3.	Crème de Noyaux	16.	Peach brandy
4.	Licorice schnapps	17.	Cherry brandy
5.	Crème de Menthe	18.	Blackberry brandy
6.	Crème de Banane	19.	Apricot brandy
7.	Maraschino liqueur	20.	Frangelico
8.	Coffee liqueur	21.	Irish Cream
9.	Blue Curaçao	22.	Kummel
10.	Apricot liqueur	23.	Peach liqueur
11.	Orange Curaçao	24.	Sloe gin
12.	Triple Sec	25.	Cream
13	Amaretto		

Carefully following a recipe might be the safest place to start. If worse comes to worst and the layers mix, stir it all together, put it in a shot glass and call it a shooter. It will probably taste just fine.

Pousse-café classics A couple of pousse-café recipes have already been given: check Chapter 9 for an **M & M** (page 101), and chapter 10 for a **Cucaracha** (page 112) and **Lizard Slime** (page 112).

For each drink layer, except for the first, pour the required liquid in a small wine or pony glass, before pouring it into the pousse-café glass. If you hold the back of a spoon a hair above the previous layer, the liquid will disperse more slowly and be more likely to float on top of the previous layer.

Angel's Delight

1/4 oz. (8 mL) grenadine
1/4 oz. (8 mL) Triple Sec
1/4 oz. (8 mL) Crème Yvette
1/4 oz. (8 mL) cream

Follow the exact order given. Pour the grenadine into a pousse-café glass. Next, pour the Triple Sec into a jigger. From the jigger, pour the Triple Sec slowly over the back of a spoon so it floats on top of the grenadine. Repeat the jigger process for the Crème Yvette and lastly, the cream.

Angel's Kiss

1/4 oz. (8 mL) white Crème de Cacao
1/4 oz. (8 mL) Crème Yvette
1/4 oz. (8 mL) cognac
1/4 oz. (8 mL) cream

Layer the ingredients in the exact order given.

 A rose by any other name...

There is a prevailing theory about drink names. Some bartenders swear that the naughtier the name, the better. Hence the popularity of drinks like Screaming Orgasm, Sex on the Beach and Between the Sheets. Sometimes gross is good too – Brain Hemorrhage or Tidy Bowl.

One pousse-café from the early 1900s involved a layer of Crème de Cacao and a layer of cream with a maraschino cherry. This was called an Angel's Tit; however, even now, the drink is frequently listed as an Angel's Tip so as not to offend.

B52

See Chapter 9 (page 97).

King Alphonse

1/2 oz. (15 mL) Crème de Cacao
1/2 oz. (15 mL) cream

With the Crème de Cacao already in the pousse-café glass, slowly pour the cream from a jigger over the back of a spoon.

King's Cup

1/2 oz. (15 mL) Galliano
1/4 oz. (8 mL) cream

As above, layer the cream on top of the Galliano.

Savoy Hotel

1/2 oz. (15 mL) white Crème de Cacao
1/2 oz. (15 mL) Bénédictine
1/2 oz. (15 mL) brandy

Layer in the exact order given, starting with the crème de cacao.

Traffic Light

1/3 oz. (10 mL) green Crème de Menthe
1/3 oz. (10 mL) Crème de Banane
1/3 oz. (10 mL) Sloe gin

As above, start with the Crème de Menthe and layer in the order given.

Yellow Morning

See Chapter 8 (page 90).

FINAL CURTAIN: SPECIAL COFFEES AND TEAS

Instead of coffee and liqueurs, another pleasant option is to serve a specialty coffee or tea, with the liquor already included.

Amaretto Café

1½ oz. (45 mL) Amaretto
hot coffee
whipped cream

Stir coffee and Amaretto together in a mug. Spoon whipped cream on top.

Calypso Coffee

1½ oz. (45 mL) Tia Maria
1/2 oz. (15 mL) dark rum
4-6 oz. (120-180 mL) hot coffee
2 oz. (60 mL) cream

In a mug or Irish coffee glass, mix the coffee, rum and Tia Maria together. Float the cream on top.

Coffee Smoothie (serves 2)

3 oz. (90 mL) coffee liqueur
1/2 cup (125 mL) cold coffee
1/2 cup (125 mL) milk
4 scoops vanilla ice cream

Place all ingredients in a blender and process until smooth.

••

A good warm-weather dessert coffee.

••

Coffee Royale

2 oz. (60 mL) brandy
4-6 oz. (120-180 mL) hot coffee
1 tsp. (5 mL) sugar
2 oz. (60 mL) heavy cream

In an Irish coffee glass, or mug, stir together coffee, brandy and sugar. Float the cream on top.

Hot Irish Tea

1½ oz. (45 mL) Irish whiskey
1 tsp. (5 mL) sugar
4-6 oz. (120-180 mL) hot tea
cinnamon stick
lemon wedge

Stir the first three ingredients together in a mug or Irish coffee glass. Serve with cinnamon stick and a lemon wedge.

Iced Irish Cappuccino

2 oz. (60 mL) Irish cream
5 oz. (150 mL) strong cold coffee
1 tsp. (5 mL) sugar
1/2 cup (125 mL) ice
whipped cream
cinnamon

Process the first four ingredients in a blender. Pour into a coffee glass or mug and top with whipped cream and a sprinkle of cinnamon.

Irish Coffee

1½ oz. (45 mL) Irish whiskey
4-6 oz. (120-180 mL) hot coffee
1 tsp. (5 mL) sugar
2 tbsp. (30 mL) whipped cream or heavy cream

Dissolve sugar in coffee. Add whiskey and top with whipped cream, or float heavy cream on top. Serve in an Irish coffee glass.

Variations: One variation reduces the whiskey to 1/2 oz. (15 mL), but adds one ounce of Irish cream. Another variation adds 1/2 oz. (15 mL) Kahlúa and an orange twist.

Jamaican Coffee

1 oz. (30 mL) Tia Maria
3/4 oz. (22 mL) rum
4-6 oz. (120-180 mL) hot coffee
whipped cream
grated nutmeg

Stir the coffee, rum and Tia Maria in a mug. Top with whipped cream and grated nutmeg.

Monastery Coffee

2 oz. (60 mL) Bénédictine
1/2 tsp. (2.5 mL) sugar
4-6 oz. (120-180 mL) hot coffee
2 oz. (60 mL) heavy cream

Dissolve the sugar in coffee and add Bénédictine. Float the cream on the top. Serve in an Irish coffee glass.

Two Irish Teas

1½ oz. (45 mL) Irish Mist or Irish cream
1 cup (250 mL) hot tea

Stir the liquor with the tea and serve in a coffee glass or mug.

Roman Coffee

1½ oz. (45 mL) Galliano
4-6 oz. (120-180 mL) hot coffee
whipped cream

Combine coffee with Galliano. Serve in a coffee glass or mug and top with whipped cream.

CHAPTER ELEVEN

Be a responsible bartender

Everyone enjoys a good time, but a good time around alcohol involves more than just one area of responsibility for the host. One clear responsibility is to make sure that those guests who are drinking alcohol are not drinking too much, especially if they are going to drive. Another responsibility is to ensure that those who do not wish to consume alcohol have something decent to drink. Equally important is the responsibility to be sure that you, as host, do not drink too much yourself. Even if you don't have to drive home, it will be difficult to stay on top of your other responsibilities.

BASIC TIPS

Under the Criminal Code of Canada it is a crime to operate any automobile, boat, railway equipment or aircraft while impaired. As with any other federal offense, a convicted impaired driver has a *criminal* record. In addition, each province imposes its own penalties, so impaired drivers may also lose their license for a certain period of time.

As the host of an impaired driver, you could be prosecuted under the provisions of a provincial Liquor Act. In Ontario, for example, the Liquor License Act includes possibilities of fines and/or prison to anyone supplying alcohol to anyone who is intoxicated, or underage (except for parents who give liquor to their own children in their own home). In addition, hosts can be civilly liable for injuries or damages that occur as a result of the alcohol they provided. This responsibility is not limited to just your party or function, but expands to include your guests' behavior *until they are sober*, no matter where they are.

Canada's Criminal Code makes it an offense to drive with a blood alcohol concentration (BAC) of greater than 0.08 percent. Provincially, police may have the right to immediately suspend the license of anyone whose BAC is above 0.05 percent. There are no loopholes here since refusing to agree to a breath or blood test is a Criminal Code offense in itself.

These penalties may seem harsh, but the fact is that impaired driving is, by a long shot, the largest single criminal cause of death and injury in Canada. The question is, then, how much alcohol is too much?

Blood alcohol concentration Undiluted alcohol can be detected in a drinker's blood five minutes after it has been swallowed. It is rapidly absorbed from the small intestine, somewhat less rapidly from the stomach and colon. The amount of alcohol required to reach the legal limit of blood alcohol concentration depends on the individual, and a variety of other factors. These factors include the drinker's size, gender, food in the stomach, body type and even genetic factors.

On average, an adult can metabolize about two-thirds of a regular serving of alcohol per hour. Contrary to what is commonly believed, no amount of food or coffee will interfere with the effects of the alcohol once it has passed into the blood.

Though there is no absolutely reliable guide, the following chart roughly indicates the number of drinks that can be consumed over a two hour period to reach a blood alcohol concentration (BAC) of 0.05 percent.

Number of drinks* in two hours

Weight	BAC 0.05%
100	1-2
120	1-2
140	1-2
160	1-2
180	2-3
200	2-3
220	2-3
240	2-3

*A regular drink is 12 oz. (375 mL) beer, 5 oz. (155 mL) wine or 1½ oz. (45 mL) liquor.

WHAT'S A HOST TO DO?

Play it safe and plan ahead. Don't offer alcohol all night. Stock up on low-alcohol and alcohol-free alternatives. Make drinks lighter with less alcohol. Many liqueurs, for example, come in non-alcohol versions, yet taste just as good (well, almost) especially in a mixed drink.

Serve lots of food, right from the beginning. It won't help drunkenness after the fact, but it could help divert everyone's attention from drinking and slow alcohol consumption down. And, make sure there are designated drivers.

Some people shouldn't drink at all

- women who are pregnant – alcohol can damage the fetus
- designated drivers – who are doing the responsible thing
- people taking medication – alcohol interferes with some antibiotics; it combines with others to create drowsiness
- recovering alcoholics – anyone trying to kick the habit with Antabuse or AA should get a non-alcoholic drink.

DESIGNATED DRIVER DRINKS: WHY?

Of course, there are many reasons why some of your guests will choose not to drink either permanently, or just for the moment. Unless the reason is obvious, like a visible pregnancy, the inclination should not really be a topic for discussion. And, certainly, no one should be pressured to try "just one." Nor should the non-drinker be made to feel like an afterthought, or not-quite-an-adult.

If everyone else is drinking Martinis in cocktail glasses, or Manhattans in old-fashioned glasses, imagine how you would feel if you were served warm cola in a plastic tumbler. Glassware and garnishes go a long way towards enhancing the appeal of alcohol-free drinks.

Aside from the obvious soft drinks and fruit juices, it is possible to concoct some pretty fancy alternatives to alcoholic drinks. Many classic cocktails lend themselves to non-alcohol versions: a Bloody Caesar becomes a **Virgin Caesar**, a Bloody Mary becomes a **Virgin**

Mary, even a Piña Colada can be served sans alcohol. Cider might be appreciated as a choice, or eggnog, in appropriate seasons. Pour chilled bottled water into a chilled cocktail glass, add a twist of lemon, and, *voilà*, you have a **Smartini**.

Here are some others:

Calf Shot

6 oz. (180 mL) beef consommé or bouillon, chilled
1/2 oz. (15 mL) lemon juice
several dashes Worcestershire sauce
celery salt (to taste)
white pepper (to taste)
horseradish (optional)

Stir well with ice and pour into a chilled old-fashioned glass.

• •

This is a liquor-free version of the classic vodka drink Bull Shot (page 61).

• •

Cranberry Collins

1/2 cup (125 mL) cranberry juice
juice of 1/2 lime
club soda to fill
lime slice
dried cranberries

Stir lime juice and cranberry juice in a highball glass filled with ice. Top up with soda. Sprinkle a couple of dried cranberries in (optional). Garnish with lime.

Down East Delight

1/2 cup (125 mL) orange juice
2 oz. (60 mL) grapefruit juice
2 oz. (60 mL) cranberry juice
1 oz. (30 mL) Orgeat (almond) syrup or honey
maraschino cherry

Vigorously shake all the liquids with cracked ice. Pour into a chilled old-fashioned glass and garnish with the cherry.

Ginger Snapper

2 oz. (60 mL) orange juice
2 oz. (60 mL) grapefruit juice
2 oz. (60 mL) cranberry juice
1 tbsp. (15 mL) ginger marmalade
1/2 tsp. (2.5 mL) freshly grated ginger
orange slice

Shake all the ingredients except the orange slice, with ice until the marmalade has dissolved. Pour into a chilled old-fashioned glass. Garnish with orange.

Keyport Mocktail

6 oz. (180 mL) clam juice or Clamato
1 oz. (30 mL) seafood cocktail sauce, or to taste
1/2 oz. (15 mL) lemon juice
several dashes Tabasco sauce
several dashes Worcestershire sauce
celery salt
lemon slice

Shake everything, except the lemon, with cracked ice. Strain into a chilled old-fashioned glass and garnish with lemon.

Kona Coast

5 oz. (150 mL) apple juice
1 oz. (30 mL) lime juice
1/4 oz. (8 mL) grenadine
2 oz. (60 mL) ginger ale

Stir the juices and grenadine together, over ice, in a highball glass. Pour in the ginger ale.

Mulled Cider

1/2 gallon (2 L) apple cider
1/2 cup (125 mL) brown sugar, or to taste
2 cinnamon sticks, broken
12 whole cloves
1 tsp. (5 mL) allspice leaves
dried apples rings
whole cinnamon sticks

Tie broken cinnamon sticks, cloves and allspice into a cheesecloth bag. Stir the sugar and cider together in a saucepan. Warm over low heat with the spice bag. Once warmed, remove the spice bag, but keep the cider warming as long as necessary. To serve, ladle into warmed cups containing an apple slice and cinnamon stick each.

•••

Especially suited to fall and winter, this combination will please drinkers and non-drinkers alike.

•••

Safe Sex on the Beach

1 oz. (30 mL) peach nectar
3 oz. (90 mL) pineapple juice
3 oz. (90 mL) orange juice

Stir with ice in a highball glass.

Shirley Temple

4 oz. (125 mL) ginger ale
1 tsp. (5 mL) grenadine
orange slice
maraschino cherry
lemon or lime twist

In an old-fashioned glass, gently stir grenadine with ginger ale and an ice cube or two. Garnish with fruit.

This is the quintessential children's mocktail. (Somewhat less known, or remembered, is the **Roy Rogers**, harking back to another era when this was the boy's mocktail. It is simply cola with a dash of grenadine, garnished with a cherry.

Virgin Bellini

3 oz. (90 mL) peach nectar, or muddle a very ripe, peeled peach
1 tsp. (5 mL) grenadine
1 oz. (30 mL) lemon juice
4 oz. (120 mL) cold club soda

Mix the peach nectar, grenadine and lemon juice together thoroughly. Pour into a champagne flute and top up with club soda. Stir very gently to combine.

FYI

- Alcohol consumption has been on the decline worldwide since the late 1980s. On the other hand, soft drink consumption has skyrocketed, along with bottled water and carbonated fruit beverages.

- Fashion is fickle. From the 1930s until the 1970s, alcohol consumption was not merely accepted by the entertainment industry, it was glamorized, even idealized. Remember The Thin Man movies, the Rat Pack, Dean Martin, Frank Sinatra, James Bond movies, to name just a few examples. By the 1980s, though, the tide had turned. Alcohol was out – sex was in, at least on the silver screen.

- You can't judge a book by its cover. Rosalind Russell once described Frank Sinatra, notorious Rat Pack leader and party animal, as "a fake drinker . . . he talks more about drinking than he actually imbibes." In many ways it is the appearance of the drink, or the apparent suave attitude of the drinker, that is paramount.

CHAPTER TWELVE

Last Call

RESOURCES

Anyone interested in pursuing the huge topic of bartending further will not be disappointed. There is a vast array of material to choose from, in a variety of formats. There are books and magazines dedicated solely to this topic. There are CD-ROMs and Web sites and government agencies all willing to share a wealth of knowledge. Current magazines, in particular, highlight popular trends.

The following lists are not exhaustive, but meant rather to show you the range of available material and spur you on to hunt for more.

Books

Something for everybody . . .

Absinthe: History in a Bottle, by Conrad Barnaby III, Chronicle Books, 1997.

Absolut Book: The Absolut Vodka Advertising Story, by Richard W. Lewis, Charles Tuttle, 1996.

Atomic Bodyslams to Whiskey Zippers: Cocktails for the 21st Century, by Adam Rocke, Surrey Books, 1997.

Atomic Cocktails: Mixed Drinks for Modern Times, by Karen Brooks (editor), Gideon Bosker and Reed Darmon, Chronicle Books, 1998.

Bartending for Dummies, by Ray Foley, IDG Books Worldwide, 1997.

Book of Sake, by Garrison, Hiroshi Kondo and George Plimpton, Kodansha, 1996.

The Book of Tequila: A Complete Guide, by Bob Emmons, Library Press (Open Court), 1997.

Bottled Wisdom: Over 1,000 Spirited Quotations and Anecdotes, by Mark A. Pollman, Wildstone Media, 1998.

Classic Cocktails of the Prohibition Era: 100 Classic Cocktail Recipes, by Philip Collins, General Pub Group, 1997.

The Classic Whiskey Handbook, by Ian Wisniewski, Lorenz Books, 1998.

The Cocktail: The Influence of Spirits on the American Psyche, by Joseph Lanza, Picador, 1995.

Cocktail: The Drinks Bible for the 21st Century, by Paul Harrington and Laura Moorhead, Viking Press, 1998.

Cocktail Nation: Cosmic Cocktails, Space Age Shots, and Other Rituals of Release for the Jaded and Refined, by Beverly West and Kim Doi, Berkeley Pub Group, 1997.

Cocktail Parties for Dummies, by Jaymz Bee with Jon Gregor, IDG Books Worldwide, 1997.

The Complete Idiot's Guide to Mixing Drinks, by The Players and Alan Axelrod, Alpha Books, 1997.

Cognac, by Axel Behrendt and Bibiana Behrendt, Abbeville Press, 1997.

The 50 Greatest Beers in the World: An Expert's Ranking of the Very Best, by Stuart A. Kallen, Citadel Press, 1996.

How to Make Quality Liqueurs & Cordials at Home, by Brent T. Huesers, Lusions Publishing, 1994.

Kindred Spirits: The Spirit Journal Guide to the World's Distilled Spirits and Fortified Wines, by F. Paul Pacult, Hyperion, 1997.

New Classic Cocktails, by Gary Regan and Mardee Haidin Regan, Macmillan, 1997.

The New Guide to Spirits and Liqueurs: The Definitive, Illustrated Reference Guide to Alcoholic-Based Drinks, by Stuart Walton, Lorenz Books, 1998.

Sex on the Beach and Other Wild Drinks!, by Kathryn Knox Soman (editor), Random House, 1997.

Shaken Not Stirred: A Celebration of the Martini, by Anistatia R. Miller and Jared M. Brown, HarperCollins, 1997.

Simply Shooters, by Eugene Coolik, Just Beverage Publications, 1998.

Spirits and Liqueurs, by Andrew Durkan, Teach Yourself Books, 1997.

The Spirits of Ireland, by Raymond Foley, Foley Books, 1998.

Still Life with Bottle: Whisky According to Ralph Steadman, by Ralph Steadman, Harcourt Brace, 1997.

Vintage Bar Ware: Identification & Value Guide, by Stephen Visakay, Collector Books, 1997.

The World Encyclopedia of Beer, by Brian Glover, Lorenz Books, 1997.

CD-ROM
Cocktail Classics (CocktailDJ)
- more than 1,000 recipes, trivia, history, myths and legends
- includes alcohol-free and low-calorie selections

The Digital Bar (Bindernagel-Ross)
- more than 1,000 recipes, preparation tips and techniques

Magazines
Bartender Magazine, Foley Publishing, P.O. Box 158, Liberty Corner, NJ 07938.

Drink, P.O. Box 1794, Mt. Pleasant, SC 29465.

Spirits & Cocktails, 2528 Elm St., Suite 100, Dallas, TX 75226.

Spirit Journal, P.O. Box 126, Wallkill, NY 12589.

Web sites Web site addresses are notoriously unstable. If these URLs are not functioning, then use a general Web search engine and search for your topic.

Bartender's Database
www.group.com/carsten/drinks.html

Bartender's Guide
www.barkeep.net/

Distilled Spirits Council of the United States (DISCUS)
www.discus.health.org/

Liquor Control Board of Ontario (LCBO)
www.lcbo.com/

Manitoba Liquor Control Commission
www.mlcc.mb.ca/

Seagram Museum (Waterloo, Ontario)
www.seagram-museum.ca/

Société des alcools du Québec
www.saq.com/

The (Un)Official Internet Bartender's Guide
tor.klippan.se/~fredrik/guide/

Vintages (LCBO)
www.vintages.com/

The Webtender
www.webtender.com/

TRENDS

As difficult as it is to predict the future, it is likely a safe bet that mixed drinks are here to stay. Certainly a look back in time points to almost constant mixing and serving of alcoholic beverages. The only real difference between our consumption now and consumption in times past is a slight shift in purpose.

Originally, liquors and the drinks that were often developed from them, were meant to treat or cure a physical illness. Long past our understanding that these drinks were not curative, there still lingered the notion that liquor was good for what ailed you. Then came the double-edged sword: while there could be some benefits to moderate consumption, alcohol itself could cause illness. Alcoholism, liver disease, brain and heart damage all put a damper on enjoying liquor. So, moving towards the future, we may still drink to feel better, but caution is a major watchword.

This caution has been reflected in generally declining liquor sales since the 1980s. Probably this will level off, yet it seems likely that cautious consumption will be with us for a while. With caution comes a desire for quality. The search for quality of life and quality time has spilled over into our interest in quality products. Premium brands are more popular than ever, almost as if people are saying, since we can't drink more, we may as well drink better.

Classics are in again, as in everything old is new again, but often with a twist. The martini has made a comeback. In fact most major North American cities have martini bars. At the very least, most major bars have martini menus, though many of these martinis are hardly classics. Fruit flavors and spices predominate the deviations.

The twist is that we want to try something quirky. Hence **Tangerine Martinis** compete with **Jell-O Shots** and **Brain Tumors**. The challenge for manufacturers and mixologists alike will be to continue to feed this Hydra-like public appetite. Luckily there is a wealth of raw material to work from. For your own bartending enjoyment, the trend should be towards whatever *you* like.

Index of drinks

OVER 100 CLASSIC COLES NOTES ARE ALSO AVAILABLE:

SHAKESPEARE

- Antony and Cleopatra
- Antony and Cleopatra Questions & Answers
- As You Like it
- Hamlet
- Hamlet in Everyday English
- Hamlet – Questions & Answers
- Julius Caesar
- Julius Caesar in Everyday English
- Julius Caesar Questions & Answers
- King Henry IV – Part 1
- King Henry V
- King Lear

- King Lear in Everyday English
- King Lear – Questions & Answers
- Macbeth
- Macbeth in Everyday English
- Macbeth – Questions & Answers
- Measure for Measure
- Merchant of Venice
- Merchant of Venice in Everyday English
- Merchant of Venice Questions & Answers
- Midsummer Night's Dream
- Midsummer Night's Dream in Everyday English
- Midsummer Night's Dream Questions & Answers

- Much Ado About Nothing
- Othello
- Othello in Everyday English
- Othello – Questions & Answers
- Richard II
- Richard III
- Romeo and Juliet
- Romeo and Juliet in Everyday English
- Romeo and Juliet Questions & Answers
- Taming of the Shrew
- Tempest
- Twelfth Night
- Winters Tale

SHAKESPEARE TOTAL STUDY ED

- Hamlet T.S.E.
- Julius Caesar T.S.E.
- King Henry IV – Part I T.S.E.

- King Lear T.S.E.
- Macbeth T.S.E.
- Merchant of Venice T.S.E.
- Othello T.S.E.

- Romeo and Juliet T.S.E.
- Taming of the Shrew T.S.E.
- Tempest T.S.E.
- Twelfth Night T.S.E.

LITERATURE AND POETRY

- Animal Farm
- Brave New World
- Catch 22
- Catcher in the Rye, Nine Stories
- Chrysalids, Day of the Triffids
- Crime and Punishment
- Crucible
- Death of a Salesman
- Diviners
- Duddy Kravitz and Other Works
- Edible Woman
- Emma
- Fahrenheit 451
- Farewell to Arms
- Fifth Business
- Glass Menagerie
- Grapes of Wrath

- Great Expectations
- Great Gatsby
- Gulliver's Travels
- Heart of Darkness
- Huckleberry Finn
- Ibsen's Works
- Iliad
- Jane Eyre
- King Oedipus, Oedipus at Colonus
- Lord of the Flies
- Lord of the Rings, Hobbit
- Man for All Seasons
- Mayor of Casterbridge
- 1984
- Odyssey
- Of Mice and Men
- Old Man and the Sea
- Oliver Twist

- One Flew Over the Cuckoos Nest
- Paradise Lost
- Pride and Prejudice
- Machiavelli's The Prince
- Pygmalion
- Scarlet Letter
- Separate Peace
- Sons and Lovers
- Stone Angel and Other Works
- Street Car Named Desire
- Surfacing
- Tale of Two Cities
- Tess of the D'Urbervilles
- To Kill a Mockingbird
- Two Solitudes
- Who Has Seen the Wind
- Wuthering Heights

Check the
following stores:

CHAPTERS

COLES

SMITHBOOKS

WORLDS BIGGEST BOOKSTORE

for our selection

THE CANTERBURY TALES

- The Canterbury Tales
- Prologue to the Canterbury Tales Total Study Edition
- Prologue to the Canterbury Tales

FRENCH

- French Grammar Questions & Answers
- French Grammar Simplified
- French Verbs Fully Conjugated
- French Verbs Simplified

CHEMISTRY

- Elementary Chemistry Notes Rev.
- How to Solve Chemistry Problems
- Introduction to Chemistry
- Senior Chemistry Notes Rev.

BIOLOGY

- Biology Notes

PHYSICS

- Elementary Physics Notes
- Senior Physics

MATHEMATICS

- Elementary Algebra Notes
- Secondary School Mathematics 1
- Secondary School Mathematics 4

REFERENCE

- Dictionary of Literary Terms
- Effective Term Papers and Reports
- English Grammar Simplified
- Handbook of English Grammar & Composition
- How to Write Good Essays & Critical Reviews
- Secrets of Studying English

**For fifty years, Coles Notes have been helping
students get through high school and university.
New Coles Notes will help get you through the rest of life.**

Look for these NEW COLES NOTES!

GETTING ALONG IN ...

- French
- Spanish
- Italian
- German
- Russian

HOW-TO ...

- Write Effective Business Letters
- Write a Great Résumé
- Do A Great Job Interview
- Start Your Own Small Business
- Buy and Sell Your Home
- Plan Your Estate

YOUR GUIDE TO ...

- Basic Investing
- Mutual Funds
- Investing in Stocks
- Speed Reading
- Public Speaking
- Wine
- Effective Business Presentations

MOMS AND DADS' GUIDE TO ...

- Basketball for Kids
- Baseball for Kids
- Soccer for Kids
- Hockey for Kids
- Gymnastics for Kids
- Martial Arts for Kids
- Helping Your Child in Math
- Raising A Reader
- Your Child: The First Year
- Your Child: The Terrific Twos
- Your Child: Age Three and Four

HOW TO GET AN A IN ...

- Sequences & Series
- Trigonometry & Circle Geometry
- Senior Algebra with Logs & Exponents
- Permutations, Combinations & Probability
- Statistics & Data Analysis
- Calculus
- Senior Physics
- Senior English Essays
- School Projects & Presentations